JUMP, I'LL CATCH YOU!

a two-character play

by

Cy Young

SAMUEL FRENCH, INC.
45 West 25th Street   NEW YORK 10010
7623 Sunset Boulevard HOLLYWOOD 90046
LONDON   TORONTO

IMPORTANT BILLING AND CREDIT REQUIREMENTS

Jump, I'll Catch You! premiered October, 1984 at the Riverwest Theatre in New York City. It was produced by CHS Productions in association with Riverwest Management Co. and directed by Loukas Skipitaris.

MERRIAM .... Sharon Ullrick
BENNIE................................ Tony Miratti

Set Design: James Noone
Lighting Design: Matt Ehlert
Costume Design: Karen Gerson
Sound Design: David Lawson
Technical Director: Christopher Cole
Stage Manager: Marcia Simon

The play was originally developed in workshop at the Mark Taper Theater in Los Angeles.

CHARACTERS

MERRIAM

BENNIE

ACT I

ACT II

PRODUCTION NOTE

Each set throughout the play is to be suggested simply, economically. Light and mobile, these few pieces will be moved swiftly into place and easily struck, possibly by the actors themselves. Focus is on the people and their relationship, not extraneum. Careful, focused lighting and unobtrusive sound effects are essential elements.

ACT I

Scene 1

SCENE: The play beings in DARKNESS. The distant sound of a BUS sneaks in. The noise grows louder as the bus approaches the audience. Gradually increasing in volume and intensity, the impersonal, raucous whine of the engine thunders toward us until the roar floods the theater. At the height of this audacious assault on our eardrums, the bus screeches to a halt, its latent power muffled to a throbbing hum as the vehicle idles. The doors air brake open.

AT RISE: LIGHTS up. A small compact area of the bus's interior is illuminated. This interior can be as simple as four stools, depending on budget. There is one passenger: an attractive WOMAN, thirty-five to forty-five, who sits bundled up in a fashionable coat/hat near the unseen bus driver down left. SHE stares forlornly out the window, a look of wistful regret etched in her face.

A chronic sense of cold isolation permeates the atmosphere. A spot picks up a MAN who runs on down right, boards the bus, drops his fare in. The doors close, the bus sputters off jerkily. The MAN and WOMAN hold on to keep their balance. We want to establish that this is a specific bus driver who drives badly: he goes too fast, swerves and makes abrupt stops.

*The MAN, who carries three roses, walks up the aisle,
pauses by the woman, then slides into the seat beside
her. SHE looks around, sees that the bus is empty, and
draws away in fear of the man.*

*HE glances at the woman, then looks away. THEY ride in
silence for a moment, the woman in dread of contact,
the man expectant of it. Finally HE turns to her and
speaks.*

MAN. (*Simply.*) I died once.

WOMAN. (*Looks at the man with a blank stare.*)
What?

MAN. I died once.

WOMAN. (*Getting up.*) Excuse me.

MAN. Where you going?

WOMAN. To a different seat. Excuse me.

MAN. I'm not crazy if that's what you're afraid of.

WOMAN. I'm not afraid of anything. This is an empty
bus, you could have sat anywhere, but you sit down by
me. Then the first thing out of your mouth is "I died
once!"

MAN. I'm sorry. I didn't mean to upset you.

WOMAN. I'm not upset. Excuse me.

MAN. Look, I like to talk to people. That's why I sat
down here. I'm not very good at starting conversations, it's
a dreary, depressing day and I didn't want to sit alone. I'll
move.

*(The MAN gets up, then sits down in a seat next to the
window across the aisle from the WOMAN who is still*

standing. The bus turns a corner too fast, the MAN and WOMAN react by leaning to the right.)

MAN. (*Looking up at the woman.*) Please sit down. It's dangerous standing on the bus.

(The WOMAN sits, thinks about what the man has said, looks over at him. SHE starts to speak, thinks better of it, turns away and looks out the window. After a pause, her curiosity gets the better of her. SHE turns to the man again.)

WOMAN. Did you really die once?
MAN. (*Turning to the woman.*) Yes, I really did.
WOMAN. (*Matter-of-fact.*) So did I.
MAN. I guess there are a lot of us.
WOMAN. (*Studying the man.*) What did you feel?
MAN. Sad. I just felt sad . . . kind of detached from everything. I was sorry I didn't do more with my life.
WOMAN. I have a close friend who survived a massive heart attack. He saw his dead wife beckoning him. He was running across a field, chasing a luminescent butterfly.
MAN. (*Simple and open.*) People have told me similar things, how they were in a new place, floating through a tunnel with light at the end or running across a field like your friend.

(SHE stares at the man without expression.)

WOMAN. (*Sotto, non-stop.*) This wasn't after death, this was before it, my friend was a butterfly collector, he was chasing a butterfly, *that's* why he had the heart attack.

MAN. Oh.

WOMAN. It was just outside of Duluth.

(*The MAN nods.*)

WOMAN. How long were you dead?

MAN. My heart stopped for two full minutes.

(*The WOMAN settles back in her seat with a smug look. It's important here to establish her competitiveness with men.*)

WOMAN. (*Slightly superior.*) Mine stopped for two-thirty-five. That's what one of the doctors said. The anesthetist clocked me at two-fifty.

MAN. (*Does not pick up on her attitude. HE remains ingenuous.*) This is quite a coincidence, you know, two people sitting next to each other on a bus find out they've both had out of body experiences.

WOMAN. (*Her face falls. SHE glances apprehensively at the man.*) I wasn't out of body.

MAN. You weren't?

WOMAN. No. I don't remember anything. Total blank. (*Afraid he's going to top her.*) *You* were out of body?

MAN. Yes. I hovered.

WOMAN. (*Envious disbelief.*) You hovered? You mean around the ceiling?

MAN. (*Pointing up.*) Around the light bulb, over the operating table. I could see everything, the sutures, the blood, the doctors . . . (*Picturing it.*) . . . there was one nurse that was very well built.

WOMAN. (*Awed.*) You noticed a busty nurse when you were out of body?

MAN. Yes. Well, I was *just* out.

WOMAN. (*Cynically.*) Could you see down her blouse?

(*Her cynicism is wasted on him.*)

MAN. (*Smiling.*) I didn't try, I was dead, I had other things on my mind.

WOMAN. You weren't dead if you were hovering around the light bulb.

MAN. My body was dead. I was a spirit.

WOMAN. (*Shifts in her seat, studying the man intensely.*) What other things did you think of?

MAN. I don't remember. I know I wanted to get back into my body . . . .

WOMAN. (*Sarcastically.*) Yes, especially once you got a look at that nurse.

MAN. (*Smiling.*) Yes.

WOMAN. Did you have any sexual urge at all?

MAN. I don't think so.

WOMAN. (*Leaning forward.*) Then why did you notice the nurse? If you were a pure spirit, you wouldn't have even noticed her.

MAN. (*Mulling this.*) I don't know . . . how do you know spirits don't do it?

WOMAN. (*Astonished at the implications.*) Have sex?

MAN. Yes. Maybe they have ways we don't even know about.

WOMAN. (*Laughs self-consciously.*) Do you know how weird this conversation is?

MAN. (*With quiet dignity.*) It's not weird. When you've died and come back, you see things on a deeper level. I appreciate things more, I cherish life. I'm not as superficial as I used to be.

(*She can't categorize this man. Her look is one of befuddlement.*)

WOMAN. How do you mean?

MAN. Well, sex, for instance. It used to drive me crazy. Now I'm not driven quite so far.

WOMAN. (*With weary resignation, forgetting that she was the first to broach the subject.*) Why is it every time a woman has a conversation with a man, the subject always gets around to sex, it never fails . . . .

MAN. (*A faraway look.*) I get lonely . . . but I know everything's going to be okay . . . in the end . . . .

WOMAN. Did you and that nurse ever get together?

MAN. (*Slight smile.*) No. I didn't even think about it until just now.

(*A beat. Up until now, the woman has been treating this man the way she would treat any strange male, with suspicion and all her defenses up. Now SHE begins to relax slightly—his innocence has affected her.*
The bus swerves over to a stop, the driver slams on the brakes. The TWO are thrown forward. After they recover, SHE looks at his flowers.)

WOMAN. (*A sincere question.*) Those three roses, for a loved one?

MAN. Yes.

WOMAN. I don't like roses.

MAN. (*Surprised.*) Why not?

WOMAN. I almost choked on one once.

MAN. (*Amused.*) You ate a rose?

WOMAN. (*Bitterly.*) I was a child. My brother dared me to do it, so I did, what did I know. I almost choked.

MAN. I ate a petal once, but not the whole rose. (*Nods to roses.*) Want a bite?

WOMAN. (*The hint of a smile.*) No, thanks.

(*A long pause. As the bus bumps along, THEY glance at each other surreptitiously when the other one isn't looking. Finally the MAN speaks.*)

MAN. (*Simply.*) Do you believe in God?

WOMAN. (*Shrugs.*) I don't go to church.

MAN. (*A hint of urgency.*) I don't either. But when I was dead, I had such a nice, warm feeling . . . like I was loved . . . like God forgave me.

WOMAN. Last time I was in church I was sexually molested.

MAN. (*Turns his head slowly to the woman.*) In church?

WOMAN. (*Relaxing more.*) Yes. I stayed after choir practice to work on my solo. The minister cornered me in a pew. He'd done it with a lot of girls . . . (*Catching herself.*) . . . I don't usually tell my life story to strangers . . .

MAN. Maybe you feel you can trust me.

WOMAN. (*Almost a blush.*) I wouldn't go that far.

MAN. (*Matter-of-fact.*) People should be able to trust each other. Children trust that Mommie and Daddy will take care of them and never let anything happen to them. It's a terrible thing to betray a trust, especially a child's.

WOMAN. (*Opens up a little more. SHE shifts position facing the man full front.*) When I was a little girl, my brother and his friend told me to jump off a cement wall by our driveway. Said they'd catch me. They didn't, I got a concussion. I've had trouble trusting men ever since.

MAN. (*In his world.*) Coming back is hard. I didn't want to face life again.

WOMAN. (*In her world.*) I just realized something. All my trouble in life has been because of men.

MAN. (*Looking at her.*) What caused you to die?

WOMAN. (*Wry smile.*) A man. I took an overdose of sleeping pills.

MAN. (*Startled. HE stares at the woman.*) Why'd you do that?

WOMAN. (*Softly.*) Lot of things. I still have some pretty bad days . . . I still struggle.

MAN. I'm sorry.

WOMAN. (*Looks away bitterly.*) Maybe that's why I didn't remember anything when I was "dead." They say suicides go straight to hell.

MAN. You don't have to go anywhere to get to hell, this can be hell right here, all the lonely, sad people.

WOMAN. Did you try to kill yourself?

MAN. (*Shaking his head solemnly.*) No, I couldn't do that. No matter how bad it gets, I think life is worth living. There's something we have to do here . . . we have to help each other . . .

WOMAN. (*A glimmer of hope.*) Do you take this bus often?

MAN. (*Nodding.*) Every Sunday. During the week I walk to work. I'm a foreman at the G.M. plant back there. How 'bout you?

(*The WOMAN looks out the window with a weary sigh. It's fogged up so SHE has to clear a place with her hand.*)

WOMAN. This is my first time, my car's in the garage, a broken water pump. Before that it was the transmission and just before that a new brake job. You people should make better cars.

MAN. What kind is it?

WOMAN. A '85 Mustang.

MAN. (*Gently.*) G.M. doesn't make Mustangs. And an '85 is a pretty old car.

WOMAN. (*Shrugs.*) Tell me about it. (*Beat.*) I really didn't want to go out today in this cold, but I had some business. I run a travel agency, a client is flying to Bermuda tonight, there was a foul up with the tickets. I'm thinking of booking myself on a flight, who needs this weather.

(*The bus comes to a railroad crossing. The timing is this: seven "dings," a beat after the last "ding," then the bus hits a bump. The WOMAN and MAN bounce up in their seats. This sequence is repeated in two other scenes and is the same each time. Dialogue should continue through this action.*)

WOMAN. What caused you to die?

MAN. (*Pauses.*) I was in an accident. We were on our way to Green Lake Wisconsin on a vacation.

WOMAN. (*A concerned look.*) Who's "we"?

MAN. My wife and two children.

WOMAN. (*Fearing the answer.*) What . . . happened to them?

MAN. (*Smiles, then softly.*) They're okay. Well, this is where I get off. Nice talking to you.

WOMAN. Likewise.

(The MAN rises and crosses downstage to the door where HE stands waiting for the bus to stop, which it does abruptly.
The WOMAN is staring out the window.)

WOMAN. (*To herself.*) This is a pretty deserted area, there's nothing out here but the cemetery . . . (*Sudden realization.*) Oh, my God.

(The door opens, the MAN waves, then gets off. A blast of cold air hits him. HE leans into the wind and exits down right. The WOMAN stares after him in shocked disbelief. The doors of the bus close and we hear it moving on as the LIGHTS dim. In the darkness the ENGINE DIMINISHES to silence.)

End of Scene 1

ACT I

Scene 2

*(In the DARKNESS between scenes one and two there is a
    short beat of silence. Then in the distance we hear the
    bus barrelling toward us. The bus ENGINE sound effect
    grows louder until it fills the theater. The driver slams
    on the brakes. TIRES SQUEAL, the bus comes to a
    stop, ENGINE idling.*
*LIGHTS up. The WOMAN is discovered sitting in the
    same seat. SHE has just been thrown forward by the
    sudden stop.*
*SHE sits up and looks daggers at the driver area. She wears
    a lighter coat indicating warmer weather.*
*It is a sunny Sunday afternoon a week later. The MAN
    runs up and boards the bus carrying three carnations.
    HE's surprised to see the WOMAN and sits beside her.)*

MAN. Car still in the garage?

WOMAN. *(Evasively.)* Oh . . . yes . . . you know how
long it takes to fix anything these days, especially a car . .
. .

*(The bus pulls quickly away from the curb, jerks several
    times, then zooms off.)*

MAN. *(Indicating himself.)* I know a good mechanic if
you need one.

WOMAN *(Eyes down.)* Thank you, I . . .

(*The WOMAN looks intensely at the man, then bursts into
    loud, uncontrolled sobs.*
The MAN stares at her dumbfounded.)

WOMAN. (*Struggling.*) I'm sorry, I'm really sorry, It's
just that, well, I've been thinking about . . . what
happened to you, you know, with your family . . . and I
realized how crass I was, thinking only of myself, and I
just . . . wanted to tell you how sorry I am . . . (*Losing
control.*) . . . and to ask you to forgive me, this is
embarrassing. (*SHE tries to cover her crying, then glances
quickly over her shoulder to indicate that other passengers
may be watching.*)

MAN. (*Seriously.*) I believe in crying. I think people
who cry a lot live longer, happier lives.

WOMAN. (*Thinks about this then looks at the man
strangely.*) That doesn't sound right.

MAN. (*Smiling.*) What I mean is it's important to be
able to let your emotions out. It's healthier.

WOMAN. (*Shakes her head, chagrined.*) If that's true, I
should be one of the healthiest people around

(*The bus turns the same corner too fast as in Scene 1—the
    MAN and WOMAN react by leaning to the right.*)

MAN. I admire people who cry.

WOMAN. (*Sniffling.*) You don't?

MAN. No.

WOMAN. But after the accident . . . didn't you . . .
well, you must have been grief stricken. You cried then,
didn't you?

MAN. No. I knew it was all right.

WOMAN. (*Looks at him skeptically.*) You didn't cry? You didn't feel anything? Loss? Bitterness? Nothing?

MAN. Oh, I felt things, I told you I was sad, but . . . I also felt . . . happy, because I realized there wasn't any death, only a different experience, and I knew Davie, Stevie and Ella were going on . . . .

(*The WOMAN cries full out again.*)

WOMAN. (*Through her tears.*) But you'll never see them again!

MAN. (*Reassuring her.*) Sure I will. Everybody sees everybody again.

(*The thought of this brings her up short. HER crying tapers off.*)

WOMAN. I sincerely hope you're wrong! There are a lot of people I don't ever want to see again, mostly men.

MAN. (*Comfortingly.*) Well, maybe you just see the people you like.

(*The WOMAN gains control of her tears, then looks for a Kleenex in her purse.*)

WOMAN. Do you go to the cemetery every Sunday?

MAN. (*Looking out the window.*) Yes. I talk to my boys and tell them what I've been doing. (*Turns to her.*) I bowl, you know.

WOMAN. No, I didn't know.

MAN. I used to take the boys all the time. I go by myself now. (*A hint of braggadocio.*) I average around one hundred fifty points a game.

WOMAN. (*Still searching for a Kleenex in her purse.*) Is that good?

MAN. (*Nodding.*) For me it is. Here. (*HE pulls out a Kleenex and hands it to her.*)

WOMAN. Thanks.

MAN. (*Looks at the flowers and holds them up.*) Carnations.

WOMAN. (*Unfolding the Kleenex.*) What happened to the roses?

MAN. (*Sincerely.*) I thought just in case I ran into you on the bus again . . . well, I know you think roses are distasteful so I got carnations.

(*The WOMAN has been dabbing at her nose with the tissue. SHE stops suddenly and looks at the man suspiciously.*)

WOMAN. Is that a joke?
MAN. What?
WOMAN. About roses being "distasteful"?

(*HE doesn't understand. Then it dawns on him that she thinks he's making fun of her.*)

MAN. Oh. You mean because you almost choked on one. No. I'm sorry.

WOMAN. (*Shrugs then presses the Kleenex to her nose a few more times.*) I can't believe you never cried, it's not natural.

MAN. That's what the doctors said. They said I was in shock.

WOMAN. When did it happen?

MAN. Last summer.

WOMAN. (*Without thinking.*) I had a rotten summer. (*Catching herself.*) See, there I go again, thinking only of myself. (*SHE looks for a place to put the used tissue.*) Does it bother you to talk about it? The accident?

MAN. No. Most people don't mention it, though.

WOMAN. Oh. (*Reluctantly.*) I have a confession to make. My car's not in the garage. I got on this bus today purposely to see you. Don't get the wrong idea. I behaved badly last week and I wanted to apologize, that's all.

MAN. (*Genuinely.*) I was hoping I'd see you again.

(*The WOMAN is still holding the tissue.*)

WOMAN. (*Amazed.*) You're kidding! After all my negatives about life . . . and men in particular?

MAN. You have a right to be angry. I think men in general are very immature.

WOMAN. I couldn't agree with you more. (*SHE surreptitiously drops the tissue on the floor and sweeps it under the seat with her foot, looking at the man all the time.*)

MAN. But then so are women.

WOMAN. Not nearly as immature as men. If women were running things there'd be a lot less war.

MAN. Probably. (*HE looks out the window.*) We're moving right along today . . . .

WOMAN. (*SHE does the same.*) Most of the snow has melted.

MAN. (*A slight pause. HE studies the woman a moment.*) Do you like chili?

WOMAN. (*HER face lights up.*) Chili may be the one thing in life I love.

MAN. You love something. There's hope.

WOMAN. The Texas kind.

MAN. Hot and greasy.

WOMAN. . . . with lots of crackers . . .

MAN. . . . and onions . . .

WOMAN. . . . and cheese . . .

MAN. . . . and ketchup.

WOMAN. (*Stares at him for a beat of silence, breaking the rhythm.*) Ketchup?

MAN. I like ketchup on chili

WOMAN. (*Shrugs.*) To each his own.

(*A CAR HORN blasts, the bus suddenly lurches to the right throwing the MAN and WOMAN together. Embarrassed, THEY disentangle themselves.*)

MAN. (*Clears his throat.*) How's the travel business?

WOMAN. Picking up. Spring it always picks up.

MAN. Several years ago, in the spring, we drove down to Chicago. An old navy buddy of mine asked me to be best man at his wedding. On the way there Ella and I were arguing about something . . . and Davie, who was just four, said, "Why don't you like Momma?" I told him that married people could argue and still like each other. He looked shocked, then he said, "You married Momma?" I said "Sure, Davie, I thought you knew!! Well, he started to cry, and when we got him quieted down, I asked him why he was crying. He looked at me with tears streaming down his face and said, "I was going to marry Momma." I told him I was sorry, then I got us all a Tasty Freeze and he forgave me.

WOMAN. (*Smiles at the story then looks off into space wistfully.*) I never had children.

MAN. (*Surprised.*) Why not?

WOMAN. (*Evasively.*) Oh you know . . .

MAN. No I don't.

WOMAN. (*Stares hard at him.*) Are you always so honest?

MAN. If I don't understand something I say so.

WOMAN. (*An amused smile.*) Honesty is not my best quality. I've been called devious and sly, often conniving and occasionally crafty. That was Larry's opinion. Of course he was a lawyer, he should know.

MAN. I've known a few lawyers like that.

WOMAN. Anyway to answer your question, Larry didn't have time for children. All he wanted was to be a senator—that's how I met him. My father worked on his campaign. I was a "sweet young thing" just out of Vassar. I became an aspiring Jackie Kennedy. We even lived in East Hampton.

MAN. Where's East Hampton?

WOMAN. Long Island. (*Caustic self-depreciation.*) It's only a few minutes from Montauk Point. If you're hysterical and driving the Lincoln a hundred miles an hour. I'd just caught ol' Lare in bed with an aerobics dancer. There's this little motel by the lighthouse . . . (*Laughs.*) . . . it was a wonderful scene. He told me he'd only married me for "political" considerations, my father had a lot of clout with the right people . . .

MAN. What did your father do?

WOMAN. He was a big muckity muck in insurance. (*Looks out the window.*) Oh. Here's the cemetery.

MAN. Want to come along?

WOMAN. Oh I don't think so. It's a very private thing . . .

MAN. I'd like you to come. Look. We who have died should stick together don't you think?

WOMAN. (*Looking out window.*) It's going to be very muddy out there . . .

MAN. I'll give you my galoshes. (*HE slips his galoshes off.*)

WOMAN. I couldn't take your galoshes . . .

MAN. Sure you can. Here I'll help you put them on. (*HE takes her foot, puts one of the galoshes on.*)

WOMAN. I don't think . . .

MAN. It's sanitary, they're only overshoes. Besides I have very clean feet.

WOMAN. I'm so glad you told me. I feel silly.

MAN. You look silly, too, but who cares. (*Finishes.*) There.

(*The bus stops abruptly, THEY rise and cross down to the door. The WOMAN stops and looks at the man with a smile.*)

WOMAN. I just realized I'm wearing the galoshes of a man whose name I don't know. I'm Merriam Wells.

BENNIE. (*Shaking hands, smiling.*) I'm Bennie Thompson.

MERRIAM. Nice to know you Bennie.

BENNIE. Nice to know you Merriam. Want to have some chili later?

MERRIAM. (*Thinks.*) Okay, but no ketchup.
BENNIE. (*Shrugs.*) To each his own.

(THEY exit. The bus drives off as the LIGHTS fade. Continue the receding BUS SOUND in the darkness, then diminish slowly and CROSS FADE into soft rock MUSIC playing on a juke box.)

End of Scene 2

ACT I

Scene 3

(LIGHTS up. A chili parlor, that evening. The set is simple and spare as was the bus set.
BENNIE and MERRIAM are discovered sitting on stools at the counter, facing front, finishing a bowl of chili. Merriam is wearing Bennie's muddy galoshes. Bennie's shoes are also muddy.)

MERRIAM. (*Fanning her mouth.*) This is *very* hot!
BENNIE. That's why I put ketchup on it.
MERRIAM. Really? Does it help?
BENNIE. Sure. Want to try it?

(HE passes the ketchup to her. MERRIAM puts ketchup on her chili, tries a bit, chews thoughtfully.)

MERRIAM. (*A revelation.*) Bennie, you know something? This is really terrible. I think your taste buds died and *didn't* come back.

(*SHE glances quickly at Bennie afraid she may have hurt him. HIS smile reassures her. SHE notices Bennie's shoes.*)

MERRIAM. I hate to tell you this, but I'm afraid your shoes will have to be recycled. I'm sorry.

BENNIE. Don't be. I'm glad you went with me.

MERRIAM. (*Increasingly charmed by his openness and lack of guile.*) You don't mind if I kid you about putting ketchup on your chili, do you?

(*BENNIE's focus has been on the chili. HE devours a cracker as HE looks up.*)

BENNIE. No. You don't mind if I kid you about your strange habits, do you?

MERRIAM. (*Suddenly on guard.*) What strange habits?

BENNIE. You eat roses and wear men's galoshes.

MERRIAM (*Laughing.*) Oh, that ...

BENNIE. Want more of anything?

MERRIAM. No thanks, I already have terminal onion breath.

BENNIE. (*Innocently.*) I know.

(*MERRIAM turns her head away from Bennie and covers her mouth.*)

BENNIE. Where'd you grow up?

MERRIAM. Westchester, New York. (*Thoughtfully*.)
My mother's buried there.

BENNIE. Were you close?

MERRIAM. Yes. Are you a native Ypsilantian?

BENNIE. Nope. My dad was transferred here from
Chicago when I was twelve. I was brought up on the
South Side. I swore I was going back someday, it didn't
work out. How'd you end up here?

MERRIAM. (*Thoughtfully*.) Well, I wanted a small
town far away from politics and ex-husband lawyers. So, I
got a map, closed my eyes and stuck my finger on a spot.

BENNIE. (*Looks at her*.) What if you'd hit Lake Erie?

MERRIAM. I'd have slid my finger to land.

BENNIE. (*Pressing the point*.) But Ypsilanti's so
small, how do you know your finger wasn't on Dexter,
Saline or Ann Arbor, you could be in the wrong place!

MERRIAM. (*Amused*.) My finger was on the *word*
Ypsilanti, not the town itself.

BENNIE. (*Thinks about that*.) Oh. (*Continues to mull
this over. HE takes a spoonful of chili, chews and thinks
some more*.) Must have been a big map, on a smaller map
your finger could have covered the whole state, I know
something about drafting . . . .

MERRIAM. (*Leans forward, arms on the table, and
patiently lays it out for him*.) Bennie, it was a random
selection, I used a road map of the United States.

BENNIE. (*Defensively*.) I'm just trying to get a picture
of how you did it.

MERRIAM. Well to be honest with you my finger was
on Lake Superior. I remembered an old college chum was
from Ypsilanti, I called her, she was in the travel business,
I bought in.

BENNIE. (*Smiling.*) You get a gold star for honesty.

MERRIAM. Thanks. (*SHE leans forward on the counter and looks at Bennie.*) Tell me something, Bennie. How can you be so unaffected by everything. Are you really?

BENNIE. Well. I do have some bad moments.

MERRIAM. (*Becomes suddenly animated and excited.*) Ah ha! I knew it! Tell me about the bad moments, that's what I want to hear about. What happens? Do you wake up in a cold sweat?

BENNIE. No.

MERRIAM. Do you suddenly stop gluing those cars together and start shaking violently?

BENNIE. Uh uh. (*Shakes his head "No."*)

MERRIAM. Well what, then?

BENNIE. (*Pointing.*) Can I have your crackers?

MERRIAM. (*Hands a package of crackers to Bennie.*) Tell me.

BENNIE. (*Dramatizing it.*) Sometimes I wake up in the middle of the night . . .

MERRIAM. Yes?

BENNIE. . . . and I stagger out of bed . . . (*Holds for effect.*)

MERRIAM. And?

BENNIE. . . . I get a peanut butter sandwich and a glass of milk and go back to bed.

(*Long beat as MERRIAM hangs suspended.*)

MERRIAM. That's it? *That's* a bad moment?

BENNIE. (*Solemnly.*) It is if I'm out of peanut butter.

(*MERRIAM laughs.*)

BENNIE. I told you, I get lonely.

MERRIAM. I certainly know that feeling. (*Confidentially.*) You know, Bennie, sometimes I wake up and there's perspiration running down my face, I start shaking, and I get so afraid, I think I'm literally going to die of fright.

BENNIE. Do you have nightmares?

MERRIAM. No, I just wake up, no reason . . . I have this overpowering sense of dread, like I'm over a deep, dark well and at any minute a hand's going to reach up and pull me down . . .

BENNIE. (*Nods in agreement.*) Does it bother you to talk about your suicide attempt?

MERRIAM. No. I have to understand it. It went against everything I believe in, it scares the hell out of me.

BENNIE. (*Takes another bite of chili, then uses the spoon to emphasize his words.*) But you didn't do it. Your instinct for survival was too strong. And it still is. You survived that bowl of chili didn't you?

MERRIAM. Only time will tell.

BENNIE. Want something else, fire hose, stomach pump?

MERRIAM. No, thanks, I'm full and very warm. (*Studying Bennie.*) Well. You certainly seem to have adjusted to your tragedy. What's your secret?

BENNIE. (*Looks around trying to locate the condiment shelf in the restaurant.*) You have to be willing to change.

MERRIAM. It's so hard.

BENNIE. No it's not. (*Pops another cracker in his mouth.*) When I came to in the hospital, I decided to get well and I did. Then I decided to move out of our house and get an apartment. Then I went back to work. Another decision, another step.

MERRIAM. (*Big sigh.*) You make it sound so simple.

(BENNIE gets up with his bowl, goes upstage center to a "counter" and adds onions to his chili.)

BENNIE. It's all in the way you think about things. For instance, most people love roses, but you hate 'em.

MERRIAM. (*Turns upstage and looks at Bennie. Defensively.*) I can't help it.

BENNIE. (*Picks up several packages of crackers and puts them on his bowl.*) Sure you can. You probably started out liking roses, then you changed to hating them, you can go back to liking them again.

MERRIAM. (*Too casually.*) What does it matter? It's a small, insignificant thing.

BENNIE. (*Crosses back down to the counter and sits.*) But roses are beautiful, how can you hate an innocent little rose?

(MERRIAM tries to stem her rising emotional tide.)

MERRIAM. (*With great effort.*) I have the right to hate roses.

BENNIE. Well sure, I guess you do, but . . .

MERRIAM. (*Explodes.*) Damn right I do! It's my choice, right here, right now, I'm a free agent, I can like roses, I can dislike roses, I can love roses, I can hate roses, and at this particular moment I hate roses! I'm an individual, I have the right to exist, I have the right to an opinion and don't criticize me for it, okay?

(BENNIE has frozen in position with a spoonful of chili halfway to his mouth. HE looks at Merriam and nods.)

MERRIAM. *(Abashed at her outburst. SHE glances at Bennie.)* Forget it. How did we get into all this?

BENNIE. I turned to you on the bus and said "I died once."

MERRIAM. *(Laughs.)* I didn't mean that far back Bennie. Look. I'm sorry I got angry I have a short fuse these days.

BENNIE. *(Confidently tapping his chest.)* It's okay. You need a new fuse you've come to the right guy.

MERRIAM. Thank you. *(A beat.)* Bennie? Since your accident have you had any . . . you know . . . social life?

BENNIE. Sure. I'm in society columns all the time: "G.M. Foreman Seen In Spare Parts Department With Brooke Shields!" Hot item.

MERRIAM. No, really.

BENNIE. I play poker with some of the guys, we have a beer after work. Bud and Shirl ask me over a lot, they're old friends . . . I work out at the gym. Pretty boring.

MERRIAM. I don't think so. *(Beat.)* Bennie? Is that a line? I died once? Is that how you meet women?

BENNIE. Nope.

MERRIAM. But why did you talk to me? Do you do that with just any woman you meet?

BENNIE. No, I've never done it before.

MERRIAM. So you really were just lonely that's all it was?

BENNIE. Okay. A few weeks ago I decided it was time to break out of my shell so I . . . when I saw you sitting on the bus I just had a strong urge to meet you.

MERRIAM. So it could have been anybody any woman at all?

BENNIE. No, you were special.

MERRIAM. I'm not special.

BENNIE. Yes you are, you're a very attractive woman you're intelligent—

MERRIAM. —No I'm not.

BENNIE. Yes you are!

MERRIAM. Well, I think I'm intelligent, but I'm not attractive.

BENNIE. You are!

MERRIAM. I'm not. (*Beat.*) Do you really think I am?

BENNIE. Yes, I know so.

MERRIAM. You're wrong. (*Quick change of subject.*) Now, I want to know what is it in you, specifically, that made you respond the way you did to your tragedy.

BENNIE. I'm not wrong.

MERRIAM. Bennie! Tell me.

BENNIE. Okay. Lego toys.

(*A beat. She's not sure she's heard him right.*)

MERRIAM. What?

BENNIE. I started building a castle with Lego toys. It was a big help, still is.

MERRIAM. (*Slaps her hand to her forehead.*) Wait'll people hear about this. Psychiatrists all over the country will be standing in unemployment lines.

BENNIE. I keep adding on to it, it's taking over my apartment. (*Beat.*) Would you like to see it? The castle?

MERRIAM. (*Cautiously.*) Yes I would but I don't know it it's a good idea.

BENNIE. Why not?

MERRIAM. Well . . .you are a man aren't you?

BENNIE. Oh. I forgot about that. (*Impish grin.*)

MERRIAM. (*Considers a moment as SHE studies Bennie.*) Can I? Trust you?

BENNIE. Probably.

MERRIAM. Well . . . all right. For a moment or two. (*SHE opens her purse, takes out a compact, examines her makeup and applies lipstick during the following.*)

BENNIE. Want any more chili?

MERRIAM. No, thanks. I would like a new mouth though, this one's temporarily malfunctioning.

BENNIE. (*Takes a sip of water, then grabs the check.*) I'll pay this and we'll go.

MERRIAM. (*Mock surprise.*) You mean they don't pay you to eat here? Just kidding, I loved it. Next time we should try that Chinese/Mexican combo, the Moo Shu Pork with refried beans.

(*THEY laugh as THEY exit. The LIGHTS dim. In the DARKNESS continue soft rock MUSIC through scene change.*)

End of Scene 3

ACT I

Scene 4

*(Later that night, Bennie's apartment, DIMLY LIT. We see
a vague mass rising from the floor down right. Also
apparent are two chairs, a small dinner table, a stereo
and several childlike paintings which hang where the
walls are suggested. There is a pile of games on the
floor near the castle.*
BENNIE and MERRIAM enter up center. BENNIE is
carrying his shoes. MERRIAM is in her stockings
having left her shoes in Bennie's galoshes in the hall.
SHE is ill at ease and stands nervously by the entrance.)*

BENNIE. Come in . . . . Now stand right there . . .
(HE indicates a point upstage left.)

MERRIAM. Why?
BENNIE. You have to have the right effect.

*(MERRIAM reluctantly lets BENNIE place her just inside
the entrance up left. HE then crosses to a "wall" upstage
right and turns on a ceiling pinpoint spot. A Shaft of
intense LIGHT springs out illumining a spectacular
castle built with Lego toys.)*

MERRIAM. (*Gasps.*) Oh, Bennie! (*Forgets her anxiety, crosses to the castle and stands staring at it in awe.*) It's magnificent! I'm moving into it tomorrow.

BENNIE. (*Crosses down to the castle.*) I'm still working on the tower.

MERRIAM. It's got everything. (*Admiring it.*)

(*BENNIE's face is beaming.*)

MERRIAM. You going to have a moat?

BENNIE. No, no moat. My castle doesn't have any barriers. It's open to anybody who wants to come in, have a ham hock and a few laughs. 'Course you can't be more than two inches tall.

(*MERRIAM reaches out to touch the castle but pulls her hands back as if it's a beautiful mirage that may burst on contact.*)

MERRIAM. (*Laughing.*) How did you decide to build this?

BENNIE. (*Straightening out a section of the tower as HE talks.*) I don't know. I started messing around one night after dinner. After awhile I couldn't wait to get home and work on it.

MERRIAM. Did you have a master plan?

BENNIE. Uh uh. Saw a castle in one of the toy stores, I copied it.

(*BENNIE crosses upstage and turns on the other LIGHTS. During the following, MERRIAM circles the castle, studying it.*)

BENNIE. Want refreshments? Some dessert?

MERRIAM. What's your liquid menu?

BENNIE. (*Takes a few steps downstage.*) V-8 juice, prune juice, orange juice, low-fat milk and . . . 'Gator Ade. Oh, and water. I have ice . . . coffee.

MERRIAM. I think I'll pass.

BENNIE. I'm not into alcohol.

MERRIAM. It's all right.

BENNIE. (*Gets an idea. HE crosses down to the games and looks in several boxes.*) On our last wedding anniversary, we had a bottle of champagne, I carved a funny little man out of the cork, you could sniff that if you want to.

MERRIAM. (*Looks over at Bennie, laughs.*) No thanks, I'm not into sniffing.

BENNIE. Neither am I. (*HE tosses the cork back into the box, closes it and drops it on the stack of games.*)

MERRIAM. (*Looking around the apartment.*) This apartment looks just like you, neat, tidy, friendly . . . . (*Back to the castle.*) How do these things work?

(*BENNIE steps around the castle, picks up a Lego piece and places it on the structure.*)

BENNIE. (*Showing her.*) Like this . . .

MERRIAM. (*Drops to her knees and picks up a piece.*) May I?

BENNIE. Sure.

(*SHE tries fitting a piece on top of the tower.*)

MERRIAM. How high is this tower going to be?

BENNIE. Sky's the limit.

(BENNIE smiles and continues to build as SHE grabs another piece and puts it on.
MERRIAM and BENNIE work in silence for a moment.)

MERRIAM. This is the first time I've been in a man's apartment since my divorce.

BENNIE. *(Nodding.)* I can tell.

MERRIAM. *(SHE eyes him curiously.)* How?

BENNIE. *(Shrugs.)* You keep eyeing the door. Any minute I expect you to sprint out of here.

MERRIAM. *(Self-conscious laugh.)* I didn't think it was that obvious. Does my nervousness bother you?

BENNIE. *(Looks around the apartment.)* No. In fact, I could help. I think I have a starting gun around here somewhere.

MERRIAM. *(With exaggerated dignity.)* Thank you, it won't be necessary.

BENNIE. *(Looks at her with an impudent grin.)* I could lock myself in the bathroom.

MERRIAM. I'm not worried about you, Bennie, I have a few . . . hang ups.

BENNIE. *(Looks at Merriam, thrusts his hands in his pockets.)* Know what I think, Merriam? I think you worry about your problems too much.

MERRIAM. Listen, fella, if I don't worry about my problems, how are they going to get solved?

BENNIE. Maybe you should listen more.

MERRIAM. (*Picks up another piece and looks at Bennie out of the corner of her eye.*) Oh yeah? Who do I listen to?

BENNIE. Thoughts that tell you the right thing to do.

(*MERRIAM looks at him skeptically.*)

BENNIE. I'll give you an example: A few weeks ago I was out in the woods with my friend C.W., we'd rented a couple of snowmobiles, we were zippin' along and we came to this flat stretch of ground. I don't know where it came from, but all of a sudden I had this strong urge to stop. C.W. almost rear-ends me. Then what we realized was we were headed right for a lake that was frozen over but the ice was too thin, it wouldn't have supported us. Want to go bowling?

MERRIAM. Bowling?

BENNIE. I go Wednesday nights at the Ypsi-Arbo Lanes on Washtanaw.

MERRIAM. How can I go bowling when I have to figure out my life?

BENNIE. You can do that between frames.

MERRIAM. I'll think about it . . . Bennie, why did you come back and your wife and boys didn't?

BENNIE. I . . .well . . . I . . . (*Mumbles something.*)

MERRIAM. Beg your pardon?

BENNIE. (*Reluctantly.*) I . . . there was a . . . voice.

MERRIAM. (*Does a slow take to him. A beat while SHE stares at Bennie.*) What?

BENNIE. I heard a voice.

MERRIAM. (*Instantly alert.*) Wait a minute! When you were out of body . . . you heard a voice?

BENNIE. Yes. We talked . . .

MERRIAM. (*Her eyes are riveted on Bennie.*) You mean you held a conversation?! Like we are now?

BENNIE. Yes. It was another being there with me and—

MERRIAM. Wait a minute! (*Incredulously.*) It wasn't just a voice? There was actually someone there?

BENNIE . . . yes . . .

MERRIAM. That's incredible! What happened?

BENNIE. . . . well, this being said, "You have to go back." And I said, "But what about Ella and the boys?" And he said, "They're fine." And I knew they were. So then I woke up in my body.

BENNIE. (*Notices MERRIAM's intense stare.*) You think I'm weird, don't you?

MERRIAM. Of course, but I like weird. (*Her eyes bore into him.*) You said "he" said. Then . . . this being was masculine?

BENNIE. I don't know . . .

MERRIAM. Was the voice soprano or bass?

BENNIE. (*Tries to recall.*) It wasn't high, I know that.

MERRIAM. Then it was deep like the one Cecil B. DeMille used in—(*Lowers her voice.*) The Ten Commandments.

BENNIE. (*Smiles.*) It was just a nice, friendly voice.

(*MERRIAM'S excitement is growing. SHE hops up and faces Bennie.*)

MERRIAM. (*Urgently.*) Did you feel you could question it?

BENNIE. I could have. I didn't want to.

MERRIAM. (*Bubbling with intensity.*) This is incredible! Let's recreate it—go back, Bennie, go back . . . close your eyes . . .

(BENNIE squints his eyes closed.)

MERRIAM. Okay, now just relax, shut out everything else . . . okay. Where are you now?

(No answer. BENNIE is getting into his concentrating.)

MERRIAM. Bennie? Come in. Are you hovering yet? Hello?

BENNIE. (*Eyes shut tight.*) I . . . I . . .

MERRIAM. Go on, go on!

BENNIE. I'm hovering.

MERRIAM. Good, stay up there! What do you see?

BENNIE. (*Squinting harder.*) I see—

MERRIAM. (*Jumps in quickly.*) —that other being?

BENNIE. (*Shaking head.*) No, the nurse.

MERRIAM. (*Jabs a finger at him.*) Forget the nurse, Bennie, nurses are a dime a dozen! We're not after the damn nurse!!

BENNIE. (*His eyes pop open. HE glances at Merriam.*) I'm just trying to recreate it.

MERRIAM. (*Beside herself.*) Okay, I'm sorry! Close your eyes!

(BENNIE does so.

MERRIAM takes a few frenetic steps away from Bennie waiting for him to get into it again. SHE turns and faces him.)

MERRIAM. Are you aware of your own spiritual being?

BENNIE. I . . . think . . . so . . . .

MERRIAM. Are you transparent?

BENNIE. I . . . don't know . . . I just . . . am . . .

MERRIAM. *(SHE presses him with great agitation.)* But what is your "am"? A . . . a beam of light, a wavering blob? *(Makes the motion of waves with her hands.)* Do you have fingers and toes?

BENNIE. *(Squinting, his head back.)* I . . . can't . . . tell . . . . WAIT A MINUTE!

(MERRIAM tenses in acute anticipation and takes a step toward Bennie.)

BENNIE. I think I'm . . . Yes. I am. I'm glowing. *(Breaks the spell and opens his eyes. Matter-of-fact.)* 'Course that could be the light bulbs, there's a lot of light over an operating—

MERRIAM. *(Jumps up and down frantically.)* Close your eyes, CLOSE YOUR EYES!! Don't lose it now, Bennie, stay with it!

(BENNIE snaps his eyes shut, squinting harder than ever.)

MERRIAM. Are you back up?

BENNIE. (*Long pause. BENNIE opens his eyes.*) Sorry, Merriam, that's all I remember. But I know I wasn't material.

MERRIAM. (*Her shoulders sag slightly.*) So your spiritual body wasn't anything like your body, no moving parts?

BENNIE. (*Smiling.*) I think it's something you have to experience.

MERRIAM. (*Crosses downstage of the castle, eyes glued to Bennie's.*) And you can't describe that other being?

BENNIE. Nope.

(*MERRIAM thinks a moment, then crosses deliberately to Bennie, takes him by the hand and leads him to the table. SHE places him in a chair, then sits across from him and continues her cross examination.*)

MERRIAM. Bennie, you've experienced something special. I have to find out why. (*Leans forward, arms on table.*) Were your parents religious?

BENNIE. (*Shaking his head seriously.*) No, they were Methodists.

MERRIAM. What do Methodists believe?

BENNIE. I never paid any attention. I'll get us som coffee.

(*BENNIE exits stage left. MERRIAM relates to him offstage.*)

MERRIAM. (*Turns around and faces up left.*) Maybe you're not as tied to the earth. Were you very sensual?

BENNIE. (*Offstage.*) Sure. I told you sex was . . .

MERRIAM. I know, it drove you crazy. Were you true to Ella?

(MERRIAM rises and crosses up left.)

BENNIE. (*Offstage.*) Yeah, I was.

MERRIAM. Before you got married, did you have a lot of sex?

BENNIE. (*Offstage.*) No. I was too shy.

(MERRIAM moves restlessly, analyzing as SHE questions Bennie, searching for an answer.)

MERRIAM. How old were you when you started?

BENNIE.(*Offstage.*) Twenty-one.

MERRIAM. (*Stops in her tracks, unbelieving.*) Twenty-one? You didn't have sex until you were *twenty-one?!*

BENNIE. (*Offstage. Beat.*) I was a slow starter.

MERRIAM. (*Nodding.*) But then you caught up . . . .

BENNIE. (*Offstage.*) Well, yeah. Then I married Ella.

MERRIAM. Ella was your first girl friend? (*SHE begins moving again.*)

BENNIE. (*Offstage.*) Yes.

(MERRIAM slowly puts it together. The implication makes her gasp.)

MERRIAM. Bennie? Does that mean . . . Ella was the only . . . .

(BENNIE appears upstage left with two coffee mugs and gives one to Merriam.)

BENNIE. *(Finger to lips.)* Don't tell anyone.

MERRIAM. *(Crosses down right to the castle, shaking her head in wonderment.)* I don't believe this. My God, Bennie, you are weird!

(BENNIE beams at her.
Suddenly it clicks into place. MERRIAM spins to face Bennie.)

MERRIAM. Wait a minute, no, wait a minute! That's it! That's the answer! Your lack of sexual promiscuity, that's got to be it, Bennie! Your moral commitment made you more spiritual! *That's* why you had that experience. *(Trying to apply this to herself.)* I've never been promiscuous either. Of course when Larry left me, I did pick up that accountant in a singles bar, but I only did it to get back at Larry. Nothing happened, I couldn't go through with it, the guy ended up doing my taxes. But the *intent* was there. I *wanted* to do it. That's why I didn't hear the voice, that's why I didn't hover, all because I lusted for a CPA! God, I'm depressed!! *(Crosses down right of the castle.)*

BENNIE. *(Crosses to stage left of the castle.)* Look, Merriam—

MERRIAM. —don't talk to me, you saint! I don't know how to act around a man who at any minute may float away and start to glow!

BENNIE. *(Laughing.)* I'm not—

MERRIAM. (*Crosses upstage right.*)—I'm getting a strong urge to run into the kitchen, grab the Wesson Oil and anoint your feet—!

BENNIE. Merriam I'm not a saint, I'm just like you are.

MERRIAM. (*Eyes to heaven.*) Thanks, Bennie.

BENNIE. It's true. There's . . . something I haven't told you about myself. I have a terrible character flaw. (*Crosses up to Merriam.*)

MERRIAM. (*Not believing him.*) Yeah? What is it?

BENNIE. It's not pleasant.

MERRIAM. (*Impatiently.*) Bennie, what is it?!

BENNIE. Okay, I'll tell you. Jazz music makes me crazy.

(*MERRIAM stares at him.*)

BENNIE. (*Nodding.*) Maynard Ferguson whips me into a frenzy.

MERRIAM. (*Trying not to smile.*) Some flaw.

BENNIE. You don't know how bad it is! You know how calm I usually am, well, jazz, it's not funny, jazz transforms me. Here, I'll show you . . . . (*BENNIE crosses upstage to the stereo and turns it on. The record is a trumpet jazz piece. Suddenly HE gets a silly look on his face.*) It's starting to happen . . .

MERRIAM. (*Resisting his humor.*) What's starting to happen?

BENNIE. The transformation, the change . . . oh oh, I feel something . . . something deep . . . it's growing . . . I'm trying to resist it but I can't . . . . (*BENNIE starts to pulsate humorously. It's his interpretation of what rhythm is.*) It's getting stronger . . . .

MERRIAM. (*Smiling reluctantly.*) You look funny.

BENNIE. Don't giggle, whatever you do, don't giggle! This is *very* serious, a giggle now could ruin my mood . . . this thing's taking me over, my body is not my own . . . (*Pulsating.*) Oh oh . . . . (*BENNIE's arm twitches. HE looks at it with a detached stare.*) Did I do that? (*HE starts moving around the apartment with an off-beat, rhythmical step.*) I have no control . . . I'm silly putty gone berserk . . . I'm a WAVERING BLOB!

(*MERRIAM has been reluctant to go with Bennie's nutzy mood. SHE starts to relax.*)

MERRIAM. (*Laughing.*) Bennie, you're crazy!

BENNIE. (*Moving his head like a pigeon and flapping his arms.*) I'm going to do it, I don't want to but I can't help myself . . . here I go . . . caught in the surge . . . I'm doing it now, here it comes . . . . THE BENNIE THOMPSON FUNK!!

(*HE does his version of a strange disco dance step, a cross between the funky chicken and someone who's got a hot coal in his shorts.*)

BENNIE. (*Shouting.*) The secret is to get loose! (*HE starts to involve Merriam in his dancing.*)

MERRIAM. I'm not a dancer.

BENNIE. (*Awkwardly.*) Watch me!

(HE leaps up making crazy contortions with his body and face. MERRIAM howls.)

MERRIAM. Ah, to hell with it. *(Shouting over the music.)* Bennie, I've made a decision!

BENNIE. What decision?

MERRIAM. *(Begins to move rhythmically.)* I'm going to have fun! No worries, no past, just fun!

BENNIE. Fun, Fun, Son-of-a-Gun! *(Dances close by Merriam, then whirls away.)*

MERRIAM. *(Gasping.)* Bennie! Your breath is overpowering!

(BENNIE is hopping around, staring at the ceiling, his eyes wild, shaking his head from side to side.)

BENNIE. So is yours! It's a new dance, let's do it, THE ONION BREATH BOOGIE!!! *(HE breaks into a crazy new step.)*

(MERRIAM dances, gets "loose," and eggs Bennie on. The record ends, SHE collapses in a chair, exhausted.)

MERRIAM. Ooooooo. I thought I was in better shape.

(BENNIE is standing center stage, puffing, a big grin on his face. HE crosses upstage and changes the record to an instrumental ballad.)

BENNIE. I jog. *(HE crosses over and plops down in the other chair across from Merriam, panting.)*

MERRIAM. I haven't had this much fun in years.

BENNIE. The fun's just starting   How 'bout some prune juice and bean dip?

MERRIAM. (*Laughs.*) No, thanks . . . I've really enjoyed myself. (*MERRIAM's starting to come down to reality. The ballad is getting to her.*)

BENNIE. (*A beat as HE looks at Merriam.*) We could play some games . . .

MERRIAM. I . . . really have to go . . .

BENNIE. (*Wistfully poignant.*) . . . I have a lot of games here . . . there's Scrabble . . . Monopoly . . . and checkers . . . Boss . . . Life . . . and here's a . . . game of Clue . . .

MERRIAM. (*Softly.*) You're a dear man.

BENNIE. (*Memories flood in.*) Submarine Search . . . Stratego . . . .

(*MERRIAM can't deal with her emotions. SHE gets up and goes to the door, looks back at BENNIE huddled in the chair, and exits.*)

BENNIE. . . . . there's magic tricks . . . and yo-yo's . . . (*Coming out of his reverie.*) Merriam?

(*HE looks around, sees that she's gone, rises, goes upstage to the castle and starts building on it as the LIGHTS dim slowly. Continue the BALLAD in the darkness, slowly FADE OUT.*)

End of Scene 4

ACT I

Scene 5

(Three days later. A bowling alley. In the DARKNESS we hear a BOWLING BALL roll down the lane and strike the pins. This is repeated a second time. The third time, the ball veers off the lane into the chute missing the pins entirely.)

MERRIAM. *(In darkness.)* Oh, no!

(LIGHTS up to reveal MERRIAM and BENNIE at the bowling alley casually dressed, wearing bowling shoes. MERRIAM faces the audience having just bowled a frame. BENNIE is standing up right, behind her, watching. The set is suggestive of the locale: the ball return chute is down left and behind Bennie is a simplified scoring stand. Up right there is a rack with bowling balls.
MERRIAM turns to Bennie with controlled politeness. Underneath SHE is seething.)

MERRIAM. *(Forced gaiety.)* Why does the ball keep doing that? Isn't the ball supposed to stay in the lane?

BENNIE. *(Cheerfully.)* Supposed to.

MERRIAM. *(Casually indicates the lane to her right. Carefully measured tone.)* His ball stays in his lane . . . *(SHE indicates the lane to her left.)* Her ball stays in her lane. Why doesn't *my* ball stay in *my* lane?

BENNIE. Well . . . .

MERRIAM. (*Sweetly.*) Every time I throw it down there it does that.

(SHE loses it briefly with the next line which is through clenched teeth.)

MERRIAM. It must be the ball. There's something wrong with my damn ball!

BENNIE. I don't think so.

MERRIAM. (*Catches herself, pulls back, and delivers the next lines with smiling sweetness.*) It must be the ball, there's nothing wrong with the lane; your ball goes straight, it *must* be the ball! I can at least throw a ball straight, give me credit for that.

BENNIE. I'll check it out. (*Crosses down left to the chute, gets Merriam's ball, rolls it around in his hands. HE looks at Merriam, then at her ball.*)

BENNIE. (*Diplomatically.*) You're right, it's defective, there's a bump on this ball. I'll get you another one.

MERRIAM. (*Vindicated, MERRIAM relaxes a little.*) See, what did I tell you . . .

(BENNIE goes up to the rack and selects an orange ball as MERRIAM crosses up to the stand and lights a cigarette. SHE comes back downstage and stares at the ten pins with chagrin.)

MERRIAM. Sorry I lost my temper, Bennie, but, well, nothing's gone right today, the computer's down, my partner's out sick with a cold and I had a lot of cancellations.

BENNIE. No problem.

MERRIAM. (*Pacing anxiously.*) And then I come here and get a malformed ball. People don't care about their workmanship anymore, it's a shame . . .

BENNIE. (*Comes back down to Merriam with the new ball. HE holds it out to her.*) Here, try this one.

(*MERRIAM is facing away from Bennie. SHE turns and sees the ball. Her control goes out the window.*)

MERRIAM. An *orange* bowling ball? I can't stand orange! It doesn't go with anything I'm wearing, it's garish, it's gross, and it's depressing. *That* is a depressing ball!

BENNIE. (*Cheerfully.*) Okay, I'll get another one.

(*BENNIE crosses back up to the rack. MERRIAM is aware that she's blown it. Her disgust with herself for losing control heightens her depression. SHE crosses upstage and places her cigarette in an ash tray. BENNIE picks up Merriam's first ball and comes downstage with it.*)

BENNIE. Try this one.

MERRIAM. (*Takes it and tests it out.*) It doesn't matter, I'm not in the mood to bowl anyway.

BENNIE. Sure you are. Now, before you start, give yourself a moment to concentrate, just stand there and focus . . .

MERRIAM. (*Irritated.*) On what? What do I focus on?

BENNIE. (*Pointing.*) The pins. See the ball going down the alley and hitting between the front pin and the one to its right. Then learn to feel the rhythm and keep it

smooth like this . . . (*BENNIE demonstrates a few times.*)
C'mon, get the rhythm . . . .

(*MERRIAM tries a few times and can't get it right.
BENNIE helps her, standing close, moving her arm and
stepping forward with her.*)

MERRIAM. I'm not very graceful . . . .
BENNIE. Go on, try it.
MERRIAM. (*Tries, then gives up. SHE crosses
upstage to the stand, puts her ball down and picks up her
cigarette.*) I think I'll finish my cigarette first.
BENNIE. Okay. (*HE crosses up to the stand and sits,
his ball on his lap.*)

(*MERRIAM begins pacing, her movements agitated, her
manner brusque. SHE glances furtively at Bennie
several times and when she speaks, her voice has an
edge.*)

MERRIAM. Don't you have moody days?
BENNIE. (*Openly.*) Nope.
MERRIAM. (*Fixing him with a disbelieving stare.*) I
don't understand that. How can you not have bad days?
Things happen, irritating things . . . Bennie, you're
abnormal.
BENNIE. (*Thinks.*) I feel okay.
MERRIAM. Isn't my mood affecting you?
BENNIE. Nope. Want a coke?
MERRIAM. (*Exasperated.*) No, I want a scotch on the
rocks, make that a double!
BENNIE. (*Cheerfully.*) Okay. Be right back.

(BENNIE exits. MERRIAM continues to pace restlessly. SHE finishes her cigarette, crosses to the rack, sees the orange bowling ball, picks it up, and looks for a place to dispose of it. Finding none, SHE glances around furtively, then rolls the ball offstage up left. MERRIAM "dusts" her hands, picks up her ball and strides to center stage with great determination. SHE studies her ball, runs her hand over it carefully to check it for "bumps." Satisfied, SHE practices the rhythm Bennie showed her, becomes angry at her awkwardness and tries again with furious intensity. MERRIAM acquires a semblance of smoothness, then stops and walks a few steps downstage with the ball.
MERRIAM carefully prepares to bowl a frame. Holding the ball near her chest, SHE closes her eyes, squints them tightly shut, opens them, takes three steps, starts to release, then at the last second loses her nerve. SHE puts the ball in the chute muttering to herself.
BENNIE bounces in with the drink.)

BENNIE. Did you practice?

MERRIAM. (*Stands slouched in deep frustration.*) I couldn't do it! I couldn't visualize the ball hitting those damn little pins, I just couldn't do it, the ball wouldn't go straight, even in my mind!

BENNIE. (*Hands her the drink.*) Don't worry about it.

MERRIAM. (*Scowling.*) I'm not worried, thank you. (*SHE takes a sip.*)

BENNIE. You don't look happy!

*(BENNIE wiggles his eyebrows at her, turns and crosses
    upstage to the rack with a jaunty air and picks up his
    ball.*
*MERRIAM walks downstage right and stands looking into
    her glass.)*

MERRIAM. I don't like to fail, Bennie, I've had too
many failures, I didn't need to add bowling to my list.

BENNIE. *(Turns to face her.)* You didn't fail, Merriam,
it takes time to get into it.

MERRIAM. Don't make excuses for me, Bennie.

BENNIE. I'm not, Merriam, I'm only . . .

MERRIAM. *(Gives up trying to control her upset.
SHE whirls around and confronts Bennie.)* Yes you are!
You're making excuses. I know you mean well but it
doesn't help me, I have to take the responsibility for my
actions and I do. If I'm going to survive, it's up to me and
me alone! *(Takes another drink.)*

BENNIE. *(Swinging his ball.)* You're being very hard
on yourself.

MERRIAM. *(Moves erratically in the downstage area,
releasing some of her stored up angst.)* I have to be,
Bennie, don't forget, I'm a single woman, I have to be
sharp. There are a lot of sharks in this pool, if I don't guard
my flanks, I may end up flankless. It's a constant battle
and I get tired of fighting, the pressure gets to be too
much. . . .

*(The orange ball rolls across stage from upstage left to
    upstage right.)*

MERRIAM. Nobody likes that damn ball! (*Suddenly grabs her head.*) Oh, no!

BENNIE. What's wrong?

MERRIAM. Oh, God . . . a headache! I get these terrible headaches. I haven't had one for months . . .

BENNIE. (*Starts toward her.*) Want an aspirin?

MERRIAM. No, I have to get home. (*Passes by Bennie, goes to the scoring stand and puts her glass down.*)

BENNIE. I'll take you.

MERRIAM. No, Bennie, I'll be all right. I have to get my shoes . . .

BENNIE. Oh, yeah. Here's the ticket.

MERRIAM. (*Taking ticket.*) Thank you, I'll be back for my purse.

(*SHE exits up right. BENNIE waits a beat, gets his bowling ball, starts to bowl a frame as MERRIAM enters upright wearing her heels. SHE crosses to the stand and picks up her purse.*)

BENNIE. Sure I can't take you home?

MERRIAM. Yes, I'll manage. Goodbye. (*SHE starts out up left.*)

MERRIAM. (*Reaches the exit, stops and turns back.*) Bennie, would you like to come over for dinner tomorrow night? I can't promise I'll be scintillating but I'm a pretty good cook. I used to be.

BENNIE. Sure, I'd love to come. What time?

MERRIAM. Eight o'clock. (*SHE writes her address on a piece of paper and hands it to Bennie.*)

BENNIE. Okay.

MERRIAM. (*Starts out, comes back a step.*) Are you Jewish?

BENNIE. No. Why?

MERRIAM. We had a wealthy dinner guest once who was going to back Larry's political career. I thought he was Italian and made lasagna with sausage. He was Jewish, only ate kosher. Larry was furious, swore he'd told me but he hadn't. That's why I always ask.

BENNIE. Oh.

(*MERRIAM's headache is growing worse. SHE turns to leave, then turns back again.*)

MERRIAM. Right after that Larry started having the affairs. I've always felt it was because of that sausage I cooked. You like chicken?

BENNIE. Yep.

MERRIAM. Okay. We'll have chicken. (*Turns to go, turns back.*) Just to be safe I'll get kosher.

(*SHE leaves. BENNIE stands with a look of puzzlement as the LIGHTS dim.*)

End of Scene 5

ACT I

Scene Six

(*The next night, Merriam's apartment. In the dark we hear an operatic recording of "Turandot." LIGHTS up to dim.*

*MERRIAM is sitting slumped on her living room
couch. Set pieces are a coffee table, a stereo stand and a
sofa. A few modern art paintings hang suspended
suggesting walls. The DOORBELL rings, MERRIAM
doesn't move. It rings again. SHE sags despondently,
then slowly rises and crosses stage left, stopping
upstage. BENNIE is off left.)*

MERRIAM. Bennie?

BENNIE. (*Offstage.*) Yep, it's me!

MERRIAM. Bennie, I . . . don't feel well. I didn't fix
dinner. I'm sorry . . .

BENNIE. (*Offstage.*) That's okay. I'm not hungry
anyway.

MERRIAM. (*Trying to be cheery.*) Call me tomorrow,
maybe we can get together then. I'm terribly sorry, I
should have called you.

BENNIE. (*Offstage.*) No problem. Sorry you don't feel
well.

*(Another pause. MERRIAM crosses back into the living
room. SHE's about to sit when BENNIE speaks.)*

BENNIE. (*Offstage.*) I brought you some candy.

MERRIAM. (*Shouting over her shoulder.*) THANK
YOU, BENNIE, THAT'S VERY THOUGHTFUL . . .

BENNIE. (*Offstage.*) Shall I leave it outside the door?
On second thought I'd better not. IT'S LADY GODIVA,
SOMEBODY MIGHT STEAL IT, IT'S $23.50 A
POUND!

MERRIAM. DO WHATEVER YOU WANT! (*Sits on
couch.*)

BENNIE. (*Offstage.*) I WANT TO SEE YOU!
(*BENNIE has to raise his voice to be heard over the recording which is reaching its dramatic climax.*) KNOW
WHAT I THINK? I THINK YOU'RE DEPRESSED. AM
I RIGHT? MERRIAM?

MERRIAM. (*Shouting over the music.*) YES,
YOU'RE RIGHT!

BENNIE. (*Offstage. Beat.*) DO YOU MIND IF I HAVE
A PIECE OF YOUR CANDY? I LIED ABOUT NOT
BEING HUNGRY.

MERRIAM. (*Rising irritation.*) GO AHEAD.

BENNIE. (*Offstage.*) DO YOU LIKE THE DARK OR
THE LIGHT?

MERRIAM. IT DOESN'T MATTER. THE LIGHT!

BENNIE. (*Offstage.*) THE LIGHT . . . OKAY. I'LL
EAT THE DARK. (*Beat.*) DO YOU LIKE HARD OR
SOFT CENTERS?

MERRIAM. (*Explodes.*) OH, GOD, BENNIE,
PLEASE GO!

BENNIE. (*Offstage.*) I CAN'T. I LEFT MY WALLET
AT HOME. ALL I HAD WAS ENOUGH TO GET OVER
HERE, I WAS GOING TO BORROW SOME CHANGE
FROM YOU!

(*MERRIAM rises with determination and strides
    purposefully off upstage left in the direction of Bennie's
    voice.*)

MERRIAM. (*Offstage.*) ALL RIGHT, BENNIE, I'LL
SEE WHAT I HAVE!

(MERRIAM reenters, turns the LIGHT on in the living room, and goes to her purse which is on the sofa.
BENNIE enters chewing a piece of chocolate and looks around tentatively. He's wearing a coat and tie and has the box of candy tucked under his arm. HE stops upstage left.)

BENNIE. *(Shouting over the music.)* THIS IS NICE!

MERRIAM. *(Digging through her purse. Shouting back.)* I DON'T SEEM TO HAVE ANY . . .

BENNIE. I DON'T NEED IT!

MERRIAM. *(Turns to face him.)* I THOUGHT YOU SAID . . . !

BENNIE. *(Looks in the direction of the stereo.)* I LIED! I THINK YOU'RE DEPRESSED AND YOU NEED COMPANY!

(The opera reaches its zenith as Bjoerling and Tibaldi simultaneously hit a high D.)

BENNIE. CAN WE TURN THAT DOWN?

MERRIAM. I'M SORRY. *(SHE crosses to the stereo and lowers the volume.)*

BENNIE. *(Counters and walks a few steps down right.)* What is that?

MERRIAM. An opera. It's called "Turandot."

BENNIE. "Turandot." It's nice. I don't go to the opera.

MERRIAM. You should. *(Crosses down slowly to above the couch struggling to control her anguish.)* Look, Bennie, I was going to change and go out shopping for our dinner but, I got home, walked in the door . . . *(Starting to cry.)* . . . and the futility of it all hit me like a sledge hammer . . . and I've been glued to this couch ever since . . . (*Turns away from Bennie.*) . . . I wish you'd go, I hate for you to see me like this . . . .

BENNIE. (*Takes a step toward her. With warmth.*) Why? Your face is beautiful no matter what's running down it, tears, mascara, rain . . . .

MERRIAM. (*Sobbing.*) When did you see me in the rain?

BENNIE. At the cemetery. Remember when it sprinkled for a few minutes?

MERRIAM. Oh.

BENNIE. (*Studies her intently.*) Did you eat anything?

MERRIAM. No.

BENNIE. Did you have lunch?

MERRIAM. I don't eat lunch.

BENNIE. You must be starved. (*Starting out.*) I'll get us some pizza.

MERRIAM. Bennie, food is the furthest thing from my mind!

BENNIE. Okay, forget food. Can I ask you a serious question?

MERRIAM. Yes.

BENNIE. It's more than serious. It's somber.

MERRIAM. (*Throws her hands up.*) Bennie!

BENNIE. Okay. Do you believe in hugging?

(*SHE looks at him blankly.*)

BENNIE. My dad was a hugger. When any of us kids got sad, he'd hug us to pieces.

MERRIAM. (*Dejected stare at the floor.*) We didn't do that.

BENNIE. I thought you could use a hug about now.

MERRIAM. (*Dabs her nose with a Kleenex.*) Oh . . . I don't know . . .

(*Bennie's sympathy touches Merriam. SHE begins to sob again, looks at Bennie, crosses to him. HE hugs her. THEY part for a moment. MERRIAM seems to have things under control. Her control is short lived. SHE suddenly wails and again goes to Bennie for solace. When her sobbing subsides, SHE breaks away, gets another Kleenex and blows her nose.*)

MERRIAM. Nose blowing is not very lady like.

BENNIE. (*Jocosely.*) Yours is!

MERRIAM. (*Laughing.*) Oh, Bennie!

BENNIE. Know what I think, Merriam? I think it's not as bad as you think it is.

MERRIAM. (*Shaking her head.*) You're right. It's worse!

BENNIE. You know what you need? A good friend. Somebody you can trust.

MERRIAM. Like who?

BENNIE. Me. You could also get a dog, they never double-cross you. 'Course you have to learn to live with slobber.

MERRIAM. (*Walks away shaking her head in disbelief.*) Bennie, I may need a lot of things, but I don't need a *dog*! You have to walk them, feed them, it's just another responsibility.

BENNIE. (*Nods merrily.*) Yep, but they love you.

MERRIAM. (*Turns to Bennie and lays it out for him with a sardonic bite.*) Bennie, I hate to tell you this, but the love of a good dog isn't going to do it for me.

BENNIE. (*Takes a step toward Merriam. His open enthusiasm is engaging.*) It's a start. Look, if a dog loves you, maybe you'd love it back. From there you could graduate to roses and even people.

MERRIAM. (*MERRIAM flares taking Bennie's statement as a criticism.*) You're presumptuous, you know that? You've only known me for a few weeks and you're telling me what's wrong with my life and what I need!

BENNIE. (*Airly.*) Crazy, isn't it?

MERRIAM. (*Over her shoulder as SHE walks away.*) Insane would be a better word!

BENNIE. Maybe. But I don't think you want to die. And it helps you want to live if you have something to love. Love is what it's all about.

MERRIAM. Don't mention love to me! Every time I've reached out for love, I've ended up with a handful of sheep dip!

BENNIE. (*Studies his nails.*) Maybe that wasn't love. . .

MERRIAM. (*Low and menacing.*) Are you telling me I don't know what love is? Are you telling me that?

BENNIE. No, I'm only—

MERRIAM. I've loved the only way I know how and that's with every fiber of my being! I gave up everything for my husband, I took care of my mother for the last six months of her life, and I did everything I could to please my father. Well, P.S.: I never pleased my father, my mother died on me and my husband couldn't have cared less! So don't tell me about love! Love has ruined my life!

BENNIE. I can't believe that.

MERRIAM. You'd better believe it! If I hadn't loved so much I'd be one hell of a lot better off today! (*Storms down right.*)

BENNIE. (*Standing center stage calmly. Thoughtfully.*) It's true you take a big chance when you commit yourself...

(*Overlapping lines.*)

MERRIAM. Hah!

BENNIE. . . . and you can get hurt, very badly, and it's hard, very hard to . . .

MERRIAM. Damn right, it's impossible!

BENNIE. . . . extend yourself, to take the trouble to care, but there are rewards.

MERRIAM. (*Shoots an icy look at Bennie.*) Name one!

BENNIE. Okay. It was hard for me to start a conversation with you on the bus, but I made the effort and look what happened, look where it's led us.

MERRIAM. (*Throws her hands in the air.*) Bennie, it's led us into this mess! We're yelling at each other and feeling miserable!

BENNIE. (*Pleasantly.*) I'm not yelling.

MERRIAM. (*Defensively.*) Of course not, you're a superior being, you're above yelling and feeling . . . up, up there somewhere . . . (*Indicates the ceiling.*) . . . *I'm* the evil one who's yelling and feeing miserable! (*Starts crying tears of frustration on the word "miserable."*)

BENNIE. (*Smiling.*) I like you even when you're yelling. If you didn't care about me, you wouldn't yell.

MERRIAM. (*Shaking her head vigorously in contradiction.*) I wouldn't, huh?!

(BENNIE picks up the box of chocolates on the couch, opens it and takes one out.)

BENNIE. Anyway, you don't love to get love back, you love because that's the only thing that makes any sense . . .

MERRIAM. *(Pacing, over her shoulder.)* Hah!

BENNIE. . . . you have to be willing to take the responsibility, to care. A lot of people don't want to and maybe that's why you run a travel agency.

(BENNIE pops the chocolate into his mouth and looks into the box for a second piece.)

MERRIAM. What? WHAT??!!

BENNIE. *(Chewing.)* You travel a lot, right?

MERRIAM. Yes? So what the hell does—

BENNIE. *(Calmly smooths the air with his hand.)* All I mean is it's easier to pack a bag and take a trip than it is to stay and work things out. *(Pointing to the chocolates.)* These are great!

MERRIAM. *(Her eyes are narrow slits. Low.)* Are you criticizing me for traveling?

BENNIE. No, I—

MERRIAM. *(All over him.)* You are! You're criticizing me for traveling, for hating roses and for not having a Goddamned dog!

BENNIE. Merriam, all I'm saying is—

MERRIAM. Listen, fella, I don't need your counseling, okay? I've been to see doctors with three Ph.Ds!!

BENNIE. *(Big smile.)* I had two years at city college.

MERRIAM.   (*Frustrated   scream.*)
AAAAHHHHGGGGGGGGGGGGGG!!!'! (*SHE stalks
into the bedroom and slams the door shut.*)

BENNIE. (*To himself.*) Business administration. (*HE
takes his shoes off, loosens his tie, turns the easy chair to
face the bedroom up right, sits in the chair, folds his arms
and leans back as the LIGHTS dim.*)

End of Scene 7

END OF ACT I

ACT II

Scene 1

(Merriam's living room four hours later. BENNIE is still seated facing the bedroom. The STEREO is playing a piece from "Carmina Burana." The music is in a minor key, heavy, modal, with a clot of solemn monks chanting in the background. BENNIE listens, tries to get with the record, then scowls. HE gets up, goes to the stereo, and changes it to an album of the Swingle Singers jazzing up Bach. HE hears MERRIAM crying in her bedroom, glances at his watch, and crosses up right.)

BENNIE. *(Calling off stage right.)* Merriam? How's it going in there?

MERRIAM. *(Offstage. Beat.)* Just great!

BENNIE. Aren't you getting tired? You've been crying for four hours. *(No answer.)* How 'bout some coffee? *(Silence.)* I'll bring you some coffee. You take cream and sugar, or Sweet 'n Low? You want it black? *(Nothing.)* Hello?

MERRIAM. *(Breezes out of the bedroom wearing a robe and heads for the kitchen up center.)* I'll get it myself, thank you.

BENNIE. Great robe!

(*MERRIAM shoots Bennie a bristling look over her shoulder as SHE whisks past him into the kitchen.*)

BENNIE. There's something cheerful about polka dots.
MERRIAM. (*Sticks her head in.*) You must be kidding.
BENNIE. (*Undaunted.*) Nope. Polka dots make me feel good. (*Merriam continues to stare.*) I guess it's because they remind me of bubbles. And the dance. The polka. Ever do the polka? (*She lets him hang.*) It's fun. But you have to wear short pants and suspenders. (*HE gives her a big smile.*)
MERRIAM. You're incredible.
BENNIE. May I use your bathroom?
MERRIAM. (*Indicating.*) Yes. Over there.

(*BENNIE raises his forefinger to indicate "thanks." HE exits up left as MERRIAM disappears into the kitchen up center.*)

BENNIE. (*Offstage.*) I like this jazzy version of Bach, too.
MERRIAM. (*Offstage.*) God, you're easy to please. You want some coffee?
BENNIE. (*Offstage.*) You have decaf?
MERRIAM. (*Offstage.*) No.
BENNIE. (*Offstage.*) Coffee's okay. Want some help?
MERRIAM. (*Offstage.*) No, Bennie, believe it or not I've made coffee before. Anyway this is instant.
BENNIE. (*Offstage.*) I love instant.
MERRIAM. (*Offstage.*) Is there anything you don't like?

(BENNIE enters. HE glances in Merriam's direction (Offstage.) HE crosses over and straightens the pillows on the couch as HE talks, placing them carefully until they're perfectly arranged.)

BENNIE. Boiled okra. It tastes okay but I can't get past the sliminess. I don't like pain very much either . . . .
MERRIAM. (*Offstage.*) Did you eat anything?
BENNIE. I had half a dozen chocolates.
MERRIAM. (*Offstage.*) I'll make you a sandwich . . . it's the least I can do, I screwed up on dinner.

(BENNIE stops and surveys his work with a critical eye. HE makes a final adjustment in the pillow arrangement.)

BENNIE. Don't worry about dinner. I could eat a sandwich. (*Cheerfully.*) Anything's okay. I like baloney, cheese, tunafish . . .

(Next, The Neat One crosses upstage, straightens the phonograph on the stand and puts the records in a tidy pile.)

BENNIE. . . . lettuce and avocado . . . egg salad, ham, BLT, all that stuff . . . Welsh rarebit . . . sure you don't want me to help?
MERRIAM. (*Offstage.*) I'm almost done.
BENNIE. Don't go to too much trouble.
MERRIAM. (*Offstage.*) Don't worry.
BENNIE. (*Studies an album cover.*) Did you go to the opera a lot?

MERRIAM. (*Offstage.*) Yes. We were subscribers at City Center, ballet, symphonies, theater, you name it, I saw it.

(*HE puts the album down and crosses up center.*)

BENNIE. (*Calling offstage.*) We saw Mickey Rooney once in a dinner theater. He dropped his pants. Ella was very impressed.

(*MERRIAM enters with a sandwich on a plate and Bennie's coffee mug. SHE stands up left studying him.*)

MERRIAM. What impressed her?
BENNIE. I think it was the fact that a man would bare himself in public.

(*SHE crosses down to the coffee table and puts Bennie's sandwich and mug down.*)

MERRIAM. She'd have been a lot more impressed with "Oh, Calcutta!"
BENNIE. I never heard of it. Was that by Rodgers and Hammerstein?
MERRIAM. (*Too weary to explain.*) Yes.

(*BENNIE crosses to the coffee table, sits cross-legged on the floor and takes a bite of his sandwich.*
During the following, MERRIAM returns to the kitchen and reappears with her coffee mug. SHE stands stage left of Bennie.)

MERRIAM. Bennie, I want you to eat your sandwich and go home. There's no reason for you to stay. I've been through this before, I'll get through it again on my own.

BENNIE. (*Chewing.*) This is interesting.

MERRIAM. (*Defensively.*) It's all I had . . .

BENNIE. (*Studying the sandwich.*) Sardines, lettuce and mustard on an English muffin. Great!

MERRIAM. I'm out of bread.

BENNIE. My compliments to the chef. (*Puts the sandwich down.*) I'm going to stay, Merriam, at least until you feel better.

MERRIAM. (*Shakes her head emphatically.*) That may be never! Look, I appreciate your offer, but . . .

BENNIE. (*Takes a sip of coffee.*) No use arguing, my mind's made up. (*Indicates his sandwich.*) That's good with coffee.

MERRIAM. You can't do this every night, Bennie!

BENNIE. Why not?

MERRIAM. (*Stares into her coffee mug.*) You have a life to live, you can't be my nursemaid. (*Looks at Bennie.*) I won't be a burden to anyone.

BENNIE. (*Shrugs.*) I'm not doing anything. The castle can wait, and you make great sandwiches. (*Looks at the sandwich curiously but doesn't pick it up.*)

MERRIAM. What time is it?

BENNIE. (*Glancing at his watch.*) Twelve thirty.

MERRIAM. You're planning to stay all night?

BENNIE. Maybe.

MERRIAM. (*Sighs.*) Bennie. (*New thought.*) Bennie, you can't stay. I don't have any peanut butter.

BENNIE. (*Stretches his legs out and leans back against the couch, his hands behind his head.*) I'll survive. I'll listen to more classical music. I feel like I'm taking a music appreciation course. (*Ticks them off on his fingers.*) I've heard Aida, Carmina Burana, the Swingle Singers singing Bach, I loved that one, and Bjoerling sings at Carnegie Hall . . . . (*HE pronounces the "J" in Bjoerling.*) Oh, and Lawrence Welk's Golden Oldies.

(*MERRIAM blushes at the mention of Lawrence Welk. SHE drops her head.*)

MERRIAM. (*Embarrassed.*) The a . . . Welk was a Christmas gift from a dear aunt, I've kept it for sentimental reasons only . . . .
BENNIE. Oh.
MERRIAM. And it's pronounced Beerling, soft "j."
BENNIE. Beerling, soft "j" Okay. I must seem pretty ignorant about music.

(*MERRIAM crosses stage right, downstage of Bennie, and sits on the end of the sofa, her legs curled up beneath her.*
BENNIE twists his head around to face her.)

MERRIAM. I must seem ignorant when it comes to cars, I'm not even sure how the wheels work.
BENNIE. That's easy what happens is—
MERRIAM. I don't want to know.

(*THEIR eyes meet. MERRIAM blushes and looks away.*)

BENNIE. Merriam? You know how easy it is to get into a rut, seeing the same people, going to the same places?

MERRIAM. So?

BENNIE. So maybe you should try something new.

MERRIAM. What'd you have in mind?

BENNIE. You could try mountain climbing learn to tie flies—

MERRIAM. —Tie flies? Tie—you mean with little tiny ropes? You mean tie their little legs together? What are you—

BENNIE. Fishermen make artificial lures to catch fish with. It's something men do, though.

MERRIAM. I can believe that.

BENNIE. That's not a good example. You could listen to Lawrence Welk.

MERRIAM. I'd rather tie flies.

BENNIE. Hey c'mon! Lots of people like Lawrence Welk.

MERRIAM. I'm sure they do, Bennie. I'm not knocking them or him he's just not my cultural preference.

BENNIE. Okay, forget Welk. How about a game of cards?

MERRIAM. Oh I don't think that's a good idea. I was pinochle champion of Westchester County . . . I made a lot of money playing cards. I finally gave it up, though. I had this thing about winning, my marriage was starting to break up and I was in pieces a lot of the time . . . my concentration was going, so thought I'd better quit while I was ahead. I haven't played for years . . . I don't know if I could play a casual game, just for fun. (*Eyes him.*) That's what you had in mind, right? A casual game?

BENNIE. Right. Look, we could start, then if you feel it's getting out of hand, we could stop.

MERRIAM. Well . . . do you play pinochle?

BENNIE. No. All I ever played was slap.

MERRIAM. (*Blank look.*) Slap? I never heard of it. How do you play it?

BENNIE. It's not your kind of game.

MERRIAM. I'll be the judge of that. How do you play it?

BENNIE. (*Repositions himself to face Merriam.*) You deal out all the cards . . .

MERRIAM. Wait a minute, show me.

(*MERRIAM reaches into her purse on the couch and pulls out a deck of cards. SHE rips off the cover, tosses it aside carelessly and sits cross-legged on the floor across from Bennie at the coffee table. SHE does a razzle-dazzle shuffle as BENNIE is clearing away his plate. HE stops and stares at her expert card-handling.*)

BENNIE. That's very good.

MERRIAM. (*Eyes Bennie as SHE does a few more shuffles. Cool.*) All right. Now. I deal out all the cards . . .

(*SHE deals two piles with lightning speed. BENNIE watches with awe.*)

BENNIE. Right. You sure you want to do this?

MERRIAM. Uh, huh.

BENNIE. Okay. All you do is . . .

MERRIAM. Uh, uh, show me.

(SHE finishes dealing, THEY pick up their cards.)

BENNIE. Don't look at them.
MERRIAM. I'm not looking.

(BENNIE and MERRIAM straighten their cards. MERRIAM finishes first and sits expectantly facing BENNIE who finally is ready.)

BENNIE. Now. I lay a card down first because you dealt . . . face up . . . in the center of the table, the discard pile . . . (*HE does so.*) The two. Now you lay a card down on top of my two, face up—
MERRIAM. (*Way ahead of him.*) I know, I know!
BENNIE. Okay, a seven. Now I lay down . . . (*Does so.*) A king. Now you . . . .

(MERRIAM lays down a card on Bennie's, HE does, SHE does, repeat the exchange for several beats. SHE stares at Bennie as THEY lay down.)

MERRIAM. Bennie, what are we doing just discarding all our cards? What kind of a game is this . . . ?
BENNIE. It's . . . (*Stops, points.*) Ah ha! Stop. See that?
MERRIAM. (*Peering at the pile.*) The jack of hearts?
BENNIE. A match. Two jacks. Whenever there's a match of any two cards, the first person to slap the pile takes it. The object is to get all the cards.

MERRIAM. (*Waits for the complexity. None is forthcoming. SHE can't believe it's that simple.*) All you do is slap when there's a match?

BENNIE. That's it.

MERRIAM. (*Subtly amused.*) It's a game of brawn, not brain.

BENNIE. (*Sense Merriam's disdain and tosses his cards on the table.*) Well, it's a kid's game. Want to play pinochle?

MERRIAM. No thanks, we'll play slap. (*Hauls the cards in quickly, shuffles and deals them out again like a pro.*)

BENNIE. You're very fast. You should do well with this game.

(*MERRIAM stops dealing and stares at Bennie intensely.*)

MERRIAM. (*The wary pro.*) Are you trying to psych me out? I'm onto all those tricks.

BENNIE. (*Simply.*) No, I'm just admiring your speed.

(*MERRIAM holds on him for a moment. SHE realizes he's sincere. THEY pick up their cards and prepare to play. MERRIAM is ready first.*)

MERRIAM. Ready?

BENNIE. Sure. You want to go first?

MERRIAM. (*Politely.*) I dealt.

BENNIE. Okay.

(*BENNIE lays a card down as MERRIAM eyes him cautiously. Then SHE lays down on top of his. It's a match. BENNIE slaps before Merriam knows what's happened.)*

MERRIAM. *(Jumps.)* Oh! *(SHE inhales/exhales deeply.)*
BENNIE. Sorry. Did I scare you?
MERRIAM. No!
BENNIE. *(Pulling the cards in.)* Were you ready?
MERRIAM. *(Controlled hostility.)* Lay down!

(BENNIE does, SHE follows. This continues for a half dozen times, BENNIE playing relaxed and easy, MERRIAM uptight. SHE sits forward in anticipation, watching each card with a life and death intensity. BENNIE lays down, it's a match. Again, BENNIE beats her to the punch.)

MERRIAM. Shit! *(SHE makes an adjustment in her position, settles in, then stares into Bennie's eyes without blinking.)*

(THEY continue. MERRIAM focuses her full attention on the cards, hypertense with expectation. On the next card SHE slaps, then quickly pulls the cards in.)

BENNIE. There's no match.
MERRIAM. *(Peeks at cards.)* So what happens, you cut off my hands and hang me upside down by my heels?
BENNIE. *(Lightly.)* Nope, there's no penalty . . .

(MERRIAM is growing more frustrated with each defeat.)

BENNIE. Is the light okay over there?
MERRIAM. (*Jumps to her feet.*) The light's fine! I can see perfectly! Don't patronize me! Lay down!

(*SHE drops back to the floor. When she is ready, BENNIE lays down. There are several more exchanges without a match.*)

BENNIE. The pile's building up, whoever gets the next match will get a lot of cards . . . .
MERRIAM. (*Slams her cards down.*) You *are* trying to psych me out! You're building it up so I'll be nervous! Well, it won't work!
BENNIE. I wasn't . . .
MERRIAM. You going to talk or play?
BENNIE. Play.

(*MERRIAM grabs her cards and resumes her intense concentration. Several more exchanges occur, then a match. MERRIAM slaps first. SHE rakes the cards in, then glowers at Bennie.*)

MERRIAM. You let me slap first.
BENNIE. No I didn't!
MERRIAM. You hesitated, I saw a split second's hesitation!
BENNIE. Well, I may have hesitated, but I didn't do it on purpose.
MERRIAM. (*Rakes the cards in confidently.*) Don't be nice to me, Bennie, I'm *not* a child who you have to let win!

BENNIE. (*Makes the boy scout sign.*) I didn't, I swear.
Boy Scout's oath.
MERRIAM. Whose turn is it?
BENNIE. Yours.

(*THEY continue. BENNIE beats Merriam three slaps in a
row and ends up with most of the cards. Her ire has
been building. Finally MERRIAM slaps before
Bennie.*)

MERRIAM. (*Exultantly.*) Hah! Beat you!! (*Grabs the
cards with relish. Arranging cards.*) I'm starting to get the
hang of it, I'm starting to feel the rhythm, timing's
everything.
BENNIE. You're doing good.
MERRIAM. For a beginner, right? That's what you
meant, didn't you? Well, don't count your chickens yet.
You have the amateur's fatal flaw, you're getting cocky. I
can see it in your face, that smug look of satisfaction, that
curled lip with the slight sneer . . . (*MERRIAM has the
smug look of satisfaction and a curled lip.*)
BENNIE. (*Feeling his face.*) Really?
MERRIAM. This game isn't over yet!
BENNIE. Merriam, this isn't a professional—
MERRIAM. Lay down!
BENNIE. (*Does so. A few more cards with no match.*)
If we were playing pinochle, you'd have the advantage.
Right?
MERRIAM. (*SHE accents her discard with an explosive
sound.*) Hah!
BENNIE. (*Relaxed.*) Okay. So I have the edge in this
game. In the pros they give handicaps . . . .

MERRIAM. (*Freezes in position and looks at Bennie with disdain.*) No handicaps, we play even steven or we don't play at all.

(*BENNIE shrugs. THEY continue. After a few exchanges, MERRIAM wins again, slapping too hard.*)

MERRIAM. (*Rubbing her hand.*) That's two in a row.

BENNIE. Hurt your hand?

MERRIAM. No, it's—Trying to soften me up, huh? (*Indicates for Bennie to continue.*)

BENNIE. (*Studying her.*) Merriam, I thought we could play a little game here and relax, have a few laughs.

MERRIAM. (*Leaning forward, tensing.*) You think McEnroe relaxes on the court? You think Guidry takes it easy on the mound?

BENNIE. No.

MERRIAM. Well neither does Wells.

BENNIE. Okay.

(*THEY continue. Two quick exchanges follow with Merriam winning a third and fourth time in a row.*)

MERRIAM. (*Slight swagger.*) I told you this game wasn't over yet. (*Setting him up.*) Shall we . . . play for money? Say . . . ten cents a card?

BENNIE. Okay.

MERRIAM. Make it a quarter. Whoever wins all the cards gets thirteen dollars—

BENNIE. Okay. Your turn.

(THEY play. Bennie wins the next exchange, then Merriam wins. The tension mounts. BENNIE straightens his pile with great care as MERRIAM counts her remaining cards. SHE lays down and waits for Bennie impatiently.)

MERRIAM. *(Sweetly.)* Would you like me to do that for you?

BENNIE. No, thanks. *(Beat.)* I have to go to the bathroom.

MERRIAM. No way, Buster, I'm on a roll!

(BENNIE shrugs. Resigned, HE lays down. THEY exchange cards, at first deliberately, then faster and faster until MERRIAM lays her last card down and BENNIE slaps it, winning the pile and the game.

There's a long pause as BENNIE straightens the deck of cards. MERRIAM sits frozen.)

BENNIE. *(Eyeing her.)* Want to play another game? You were just learning with this one . . .

MERRIAM. *(Dazed.)* Cards are my game.

BENNIE. Why don't you teach me to—

MERRIAM. It's the one place I excel. Excelled.

BENNIE. Want to play some poker?

MERRIAM. It was an oasis in the desert of my failure.

BENNIE. How about . . . black jack . . . let's see . . .

MERRIAM. If I can't win at cards . . .

BENNIE. Want to tell ghost stories?

MERRIAM. . . . . if I can't win a stupid kid's game of cards, what's left for me?

BENNIE. *(Places the cards on the table.)* Merriam . . .

MERRIAM. (*Building.*) What further humiliation does life hold for Merriam Wells? She's just been massacred in slap! (*SHE begins to wail on the word "slap," then collapses on the floor, crying and pounding on it with her fists.*)

BENNIE. Want some coffee, a different record . . .

MERRIAM. *Maybe that's my lesson, my last vestige of pride has just blown up in my face. I was proud, now even that's been taken away!* (In the middle of a huge sob, MERRIAM suddenly stands up, cuts the sob, composes herself, *gets her purse from the sofa, goes to Bennie and gives a him a bill.*)

BENNIE. I don't have any change.

MERRIAM. Keep it!

BENNIE. I will not! You owe thirteen dollars, that's all. This is a twenty. (*BENNIE puts the twenty down on the table.*)

MERRIAM. I'd rather you owe me seven dollars than me owe you thirteen. Don't you have any bills?

BENNIE. Yeah, a twenty.

MERRIAM. (*Disappears into her bedroom and reappears almost instantly with a huge jar of pennies which SHE proceeds to dump onto the coffee table.*) That was thirteen dollars I owe you. (*Begins counting them out.*)

BENNIE. (*Alarmed.*) Merriam? I don't want your pennies. Thirteen dollars, do you know how many that is?

MERRIAM. You should have thought of that when you beat me . . . (*Sorting.*) . . . I have ten packages, that's six dollars. I still owe you seven. *(Counting.)*

BENNIE. (*Folding his arms.*) I won't accept them.

MERRIAM. You must. It's the manly thing to do.

BENNIE. It is?

MERRIAM. Yes. "He who does not accept monies due him shall end up in a deep, dark pit." Proverbs. (*Pushes them into a pile.*)

BENNIE. Yeah. It's like that thing from Psalms that goes "She who can't lose a game of slap without getting mad shall trot alone."

(*Silence while MERRIAM counts, neatly arranging the pennies into piles.*)

BENNIE. Okay, you've got a point. I'm sorry I suggested the card game, I just got caught up in it.

MERRIAM. I understand. Three hundred. (*Pushes them into a pile.*)

BENNIE. (*Stares at Merriam, goes to the coffee table and starts putting the pennies into his pockets.*) Don't you have any more penny wrappers?

MERRIAM. Nope.

MERRIAM. (*Counting.*) Eighty, ninety, one hundred. There. Seven plus six is thirteen. That's it. Eleven hundred pennies. I estimated some of this so when you get home, if the count is off, bill me.

BENNIE. Merriam!

MERRIAM. All right, call me. You'd better get your coat, you'll need all the pockets you can get.

BENNIE. (*Gets his coat and puts it on.*) You throwing me out?

MERRIAM. I've got to go to bed.

BENNIE. (*Finishes scooping the pennies into his pockets and puts the last remaining coins in his hat.*) I noticed some pills in your medicine cabinet.

MERRIAM. Diet pills.
BENNIE. I'll call you. (*Clanking to the door.*) I could get arrested.

(*BENNIE goes out. MERRIAM begins putting the remaining pennies back in the jar. A beat . . . then we hear the offstage SOUND of hundreds of pennies dropping to the hall floor.*)

BENNIE. (*Offstage.*) Great.

(*MERRIAM looks offstage, then goes back to putting the pennies in the jar. Suddenly SHE stops, looks at the cards, picks them up and begins practicing slap with grim determination as the LIGHTS dim to black. Merriam's slapping blends with a drum slap on a trumpet jazz piece . . . We also hear the SOUND of the bowling alley . . . and we blend it all in a recording of "Aida."*
A beat. LIGHTS up on BENNIE in a SPOT. HE picks up the phone and dials.
LIGHTS up on the phone in Merriam's apartment which is ringing. A recording is heard that says:)

MERRIAM. (*Voice over.*) You've reached Merriam Wells . . . (*A squeaking noise.*) . . . Ignore that, I've been having trouble with this stupid machine. If Bennie Thompson the card shark calls, "she who trots alone" is involved in a project and won't be available for a few days . . . I'm sure you're dying to know what this project is. This vital information will soon be revealed by "she who trots."

See you soon. By the way, I'll be running in the third race at Pimlico . . . (*There's a high beep.*)

BENNIE. (*Into receiver.*) It's me again . . . Merriam, I'd like to see you . . . call me . . . I'm anxious to find out what this project is . . . oh, and by the way, what odds are you giving?

(*The "Aida" recording up as the LIGHTS dim to black.*)

End of Scene 1

ACT II

Scene 2

(*Two weeks later. BENNIE is discovered in his shorts ironing his pants. HE takes great care with each stroke, a very methodical ironer.*
There's a KNOCK on the door.)

MERRIAM. (*Offstage.*) Bennie, it's me! Open up!

BENNIE. Oh. Hi, Merriam. Hold on! (*Quickly finishes his ironing job, shakes his pants out and slips them on. HE walks over to the door zipping up his fly.*)

MERRIAM. (*Offstage.*) Come on, Bennie, what are you doing?

BENNIE. I was ironing my pants!

(HE arrives at the door and opens it. MERRIAM hurries past him into the apartment. SHE carries a brown paper bag, a tote bag and her purse. She's dressed in black slacks, heels, and looks terrific. SHE places the brown paper sack on the table, drops her tote bag by the chair. SHE crosses back to BENNIE still at the door, grabs his hand, leads him to the table and sits him down. SHE reaches into her tote bag and takes out a deck of cards, gives Bennie half of them. Without a word THEY begin playing slap. THEY play quickly with MERRIAM always slapping first and beating Bennie.)

BENNIE. You've been practicing.

MERRIAM. Uh huh . . .

BENNIE. You're the fastest slapper in the North. Is this the project you—

MERRIAM.—Part of it . . . *(Slaps.)*

BENNIE. *(Indicating the sack.)* What's in the sack?

MERRIAM. Your dinner. The one I didn't cook.

BENNIE. Oh. *(Beat.)* Smells good What is—

MERRIAM. —Chicken Maximillian. Orange chicken.

BENNIE. I love—

MERRIAM. —there's also rice, broccoli with cheese sauce, cheddar, and a piece of home made carrot cake.

BENNIE. Carrot cake just happens to be my fav—

MERRIAM. It took four large carrots, shredded, I shredded my finger in the process but it was a small price to pay for this guilt I've been living with ever since my debacle . . . *(Slaps.)*

BENNIE. Merriam, it wasn't a debacle, I enjoyed being with you.

MERRIAM. Sure.

BENNIE. I did

MERRIAM. How could you have enjoyed it? I invite you over, ruin your evening, then send you home buried in pennies! I acted like a petulant little kid . . .

BENNIE. I've been trying to reach you.

MERRIAM. I know . . . (*Slaps.*)

(*MERRIAM stops playing, drops her head for a moment, then tosses her cards onto the table.*)

MERRIAM. What am I doing? Why am I so competitive? You know why you haven't been able to reach me? Because I've spent every free waking minute over the past two weeks working on slap and bowling . . .

BENNIE. Bowling too?

MERRIAM. Yes. I bought my own ball, shoes, ball bag, had a few lessons from a pro on the other side of town, when I wasn't bowling I was slapping, my hand is chopped meat, I've been acting like a maniac! And I'm sick of it! All my life I've been plagued with this thing of having to be the best in everything I do, it's driven me crazy and I'm not doing it anymore, I quit!

BENNIE. So do I.

(*BENNIE tosses his cards onto the table. THEY look at each other a beat, then begin to laugh.*)

MERRIAM. (*Gets a tape from her tote.*) I want to play something for you. (*SHE crosses to the tape deck and slips the cassette in. A Lawrence Welk polka begins to play.*) It wasn't easy, but I learned to love this guy! Especially this one. It doesn't have the subtle beauty of a Brahms

Concerto or the eclectic romanticism of the Renaissance Polyphonists, but it's got one hell of a beat!

BENNIE. The Lawrence Welk lovers of the country salute you! Wanna polka?

MERRIAM. No. I'm not wearing short pants and suspenders.

BENNIE. You're right. (*Takes the tape out.*) I'm starving, let's eat.

MERRIAM. You go ahead, I'm not hungry.

BENNIE. I'm not either, I lied.

(*THEY look at each other.*)

BENNIE. Learn to like roses yet?

MERRIAM. I don't know . . .

BENNIE. Well, it's a little, insignificant thing . . .

MERRIAM. Sometimes it's those insignificant things that could make the difference, one way or the other.

BENNIE. What do you mean?

MERRIAM. The day mother died, my father wanted me to go home from the cemetery with him but I hated him at that moment and blamed him for my mother's death . . . so a friend took me home and I decided to go for a drive by myself. So. I'm in my car and, by the way, it's raining, get the picture? And I end up going across the George Washington Bridge toward New Jersey. So, as I'm jockeying for position to get into the fast lane, a panel truck with Jersey plates zooms across three lanes and cuts me off. I honk my horn and he gives me the finger. So what does any good New Yorker do? I roll down my window and call him a part of his anatomy he's never faced. It was an ugly scene. I got even more depressed,

went home and two weeks later I took the big swallow.
Now I won't say that getting the finger from a jerk from
Jersey was the proverbial last straw, but it helped . . .

BENNIE. That's profound.

MERRIAM. Sure. I'm deep.

BENNIE. I missed you.

MERRIAM. No you didn't.

BENNIE. Yes, I did.

MERRIAM. No you didn't.

BENNIE. Merriam, I can miss you if I want to, it's my
choice, right here, right now and I choose to miss you and
don't criticize me for it, okay?

MERRIAM. Touché. Did you really miss me?

BENNIE. I really did.

MERRIAM. You mean all that time I was bowling and
slapping by myself we could have been doing it together?

BENNIE. Yep.

(Long look at other.)

MERRIAM. Bennie, would you come here and kiss
me?

BENNIE. *(Goes to her.)* Does it bother you that I'm
short?

MERRIAM. You haven't heard me complain yet, have
you?

BENNIE. Nope.

MERRIAM. Nope.

*(THEY kiss. It's a long, sweet kiss, not a passionate one
   at first, then when it becomes passionate, BENNIE
   breaks it.)*

MERRIAM. You okay?

BENNIE. Oh, sure, I . . . (*HE walks a few steps downstage and stands staring at the castle. After a beat, HE smiles.*)

MERRIAM. What are you smiling about?

BENNIE. (*Blushes.*) Oh, nothing.

MERRIAM. Tell me, Bennie, I want to know.

(*BENNIE looks at her, then back at the castle. HE picks up a Lego piece and fiddles with it.*)

MERRIAM. Please. Tell me.

BENNIE. (*Slow, halting, remembering.*) I was just remembering . . . the first time I kissed Ella. We were fourteen . . . in junior high school . . . I'd known her for two years . . . we'd met in grade school . . . anyway it was after football practice, I was on the team . . . played tailback . . . and she'd been watching from a little hill by the football field with a girl friend . . . we'd been friends but that was all . . .

(*The LIGHTS begins to dim slowly as a SPOT sneaks up on BENNIE. MERRIAM stands listening. As SHE listens, her body sags and her head drops.*)

BENNIE. . . . after practice, I went back to school with the team and changed clothes . . . I lived on 62nd Street, just the other side of the field . . . and when I came over the little hill on my way home, Ella was there by herself . . . just sitting there looking up at the sky . . . I remember

how beautiful it was, it had rained earlier and everything
had a . . . glow, a bright kind of . . . shimmering . . .

*(The LIGHTS are quite dim onstage now while the SPOT
on BENNIE is nearly full. MERRIAM slowly steps
back into the shadows and disappears as the SPOT
grows to full brightness on BENNIE's shining face.)*

BENNIE. . . . and I said "Hi" and sat down beside her . .
. and we just looked at the sky . . . *(BENNIE's been
building on the castle. Now HE stops, lifts his head and
stares off into the past, a look of wonder in his eyes.)* . . .
the clouds were actually pink . . . we couldn't get over that
. . . and I took her hand . . . and she . . . *(Laughs,
remembering.)* . . . squeezed my hand back . . . and I
looked at her . . . and she was looking at me . . .

(The SPOT starts to slowly fade.)

BENNIE. . . . her face was like a child's . . . her face
was just . . . shining . . . her face was . . .

*(BENNIE should have tears running down his cheeks. No
sobs, only tears as HE remembers . . . as over the last
few sentences, we've heard the bus SOUND EFFECTS
sneak in, at first inaudibly, then louder until the sound
fills the theater.)*

End of Scene 2

ACT II

Scene 3

(June, eight weeks later. Hold in DARKNESS for a moment. Continue bus SOUND EFFECTS from the preceding scene.

The driver slams on the brakes suddenly. As the bus doors open and the engine idles, LIGHTS up.

MERRIAM is sitting on the left side of the bus dressed casually in a sleeveless blouse and slacks. Her attire is noticeably more summery than in the last scene. She's taken the bus for the express purpose of seeing Bennie again.

BENNIE runs up and boards the bus. He's come hoping to see Merriam. He's wearing a short-sleeved shirt, baseball cap and jeans. HE carries three roses. HE drops his fare in, sees Merriam, smiles and sits stage right across the aisle from her.)

BENNIE. (*A beat.*) Finally had myself a good cry.

MERRIAM. Really?

BENNIE. Yep. Surprised you didn't hear about it, it was on the late news . . .

MERRIAM. Who was it that said, "People who cry a lot live longer, happier lives"?

BENNIE. Probably some great man.

MERRIAM. Probably.

(The bus pulls away quickly, BENNIE and MERRIAM are thrown back in their seats. Several beats go by before they make contact again.)

BENNIE. The dinner was great.

MERRIAM. What dinner?

BENNIE. The one you brought to my apartment.

MERRIAM. Oh. I'd forgotten all about it . . . (*She hasn't.*)

BENNIE. Especially liked the carrot cake. How's your finger?

MERRIAM. (*Laughs.*) Oh. That healed up weeks ago. (*Holds up her forefinger.*)

(*Awkward pause.*)

BENNIE. Wish you'd stayed and had dinner with me. I looked around and you were gone.

MERRIAM. Well, I felt it best, under the circumstances . . .

BENNIE. Oh . . .

(*Silence.*)

BENNIE. Merriam, it's my turn to apologize, I shouldn't have brought that up, you know, about Ella . . . I just—

MERRIAM. —Bennie, it's okay, I understand, you couldn't help thinking about her, after all, you spent your whole life with her, you can't just . . . drop all that and forget it.

(*Silence.*)

BENNIE. Finally got another car. It's the first one I've had since—

MERRIAM. —That's wonderful, Bennie. What kind?

BENNIE. Olds. Thought it was about time. It's a good car.

MERRIAM. So I've heard.

(MERRIAM looks out the window nervously as BENNIE fiddles with his roses.)

MERRIAM. How's the castle?

BENNIE. I gave it away.

MERRIAM. Bennie!

BENNIE. Yep. There's a day care center a few blocks from where I live. Gave 'em the boys' games, too. Should have done it a long time ago.

MERRIAM. Well, I'm sure it wasn't easy for you.

(The bus turns the corner too fast. BENNIE and MERRIAM lean to the right. THEY ride in silence for a moment. MERRIAM is staring at her hands.)

MERRIAM. Bennie, I want you to know something. I've been thinking a lot about what you said, about learning to like myself, to forgive myself. I've been working on that . . .

BENNIE. I'm glad, Merriam.

MERRIAM. And I'm listening for those thoughts you mentioned.

BENNIE. Anything coming through?

MERRIAM. Yes. There's a lot of static, but it occurred to me that a pet might not be a bad idea . . . I wasn't ready for the giant responsibility of owning a dog, so I started small.

BENNIE. A gerbil?

MERRIAM. (*Laughs.*) Not that small. A cat. I got a cat. A stray kitten, actually, with a mangled tail. It was that tail that got me. It's straightening out now and she's beautiful.

BENNIE. That's great, Merriam. Sounds like you're on your way.

MERRIAM. Yes, I am . . . (*Throw this away.*) . . . in more ways than one.

BENNIE. What do you mean?

MERRIAM. I'm moving back to Westchester. I leave tomorrow afternoon at three o'clock.

BENNIE. (*Dismayed.*) Why?

MERRIAM. I realized I'd had enough of small town life. Everything's been . . . up in the air all these weeks, so I sold out to my partner.

BENNIE. (*Staring intently at Merriam. HE begins fishing in his back pocket.*) I was just going to ask you . . . (*Takes out a flyer.*) . . . if you wanted . . . a, there's a Hindu philosopher who's giving a lecture next week on TM, I thought maybe we could both learn something . . . like how to pronounce his name . . . (*Studying flyer.*) . . . Doctor S-u-j-u-h-a-t-r-i-c-r-a . . .

MERRIAM. I can't Bennie, I've been through TM, EST, The Fat Lady, The Mud Baths of Mexico, Nautilus, none of it did me any good. I have learned that changing the outside doesn't make it. Something has to change inside, otherwise we go on making the same mistakes forever. But you go, maybe it will help. Anyway, I'll be gone . . .

BENNIE. Tomorrow? Three o'clock?

MERRIAM. Yes.

BENNIE. I'm glad we ran into each other.

MERRIAM. (*Too brightly.*) So am I. I wanted to call you so many times, but I thought I should wait for you to call . . . and when you didn't, I decided you were having trouble with our . . . relationship and . . .

BENNIE. (*Looks at Merriam in astonishment.*) I *did* call, Merriam, I tried to get you at home nights but you were never there! Your machine wasn't on . . .

MERRIAM. It's been broken, I haven't had time to get it fixed, I've been getting home late, this is our busy season, I've been working all hours . . .

BENNIE. That's what I figured, so I called you at work, I left a message with someone there—

MERRIAM. —I never got it!

BENNIE. —but, okay, that's why you never called me back, so I dropped by and you weren't there . . .

MERRIAM. (*Throws her hands in the air.*) I was out of town for a few days, Felice is such a scatterbrain, she does this to me all the time, people call and I don't get the message. Damn! I'm sorry, Bennie. (*Brightening.*) Did you really call, did you really come by?

BENNIE. Yes I did!

MERRIAM. Oh, that makes me feel a lot better, Bennie, a *lot* better!

BENNIE. I'm having trouble, Merriam.

MERRIAM. Why?

BENNIE. Well, you're leaving and I . . . I don't know, I just . . . wasn't ready for it . . .

MERRIAM. When I didn't hear from you, I assumed you didn't want to continue our relationship . . .

BENNIE. (*Looks at her in astonishment.*) How can you say that, Merriam? Do you think I'd buy Lady Godiva chocolates and sit up all night listening to boring music for just anybody?

MERRIAM. It's Godiva chocolates, not *Lady* Godiva, and I thought you liked the music!

BENNIE. I liked *Aida* and *Turandot,* I did not like *Carmina Burana,* it depressed the hell out of me! But I listened to it! I ate that sandwich you fixed for me, that was probably the worst sandwich I've ever had!

MERRIAM. You lied! You said it was wonderful!

BENNIE. Merriam, I couldn't tell a potential suicide she'd just made a rotten sandwich!

MERRIAM. I didn't have any food in the house, I told you that!

BENNIE. Merriam, the sandwich isn't important . . .

MERRIAM. It is to me! When I do something, I give it everything I've got, whether it's cooking, playing cards—

BENNIE. —Yes I know, you're intense, Merriam, nothing is ever casual with you!

(*The "Ding, Ding" of the railroad crossing is heard for the third time. Due to prior conditioning, MERRIAM and BENNIE automatically grab hold of the seat in anticipation of the coming bump without interrupting their argument.*)

MERRIAM. What's wrong with being intense? I feel things deeply, I'm glad I do, no matter how much I improve, I hope I never lose my zest, my energy, my flare for the dramatic! I never want to be placid and boring—

BENNIE. Like me, you think I'm placid and boring—
MERRIAM. —I didn't say that!
BENNIE. You were thinking it!
MERRIAM. Don't tell me what I'm thinking!
BENNIE. (*Suddenly breaks into a big smile.*) Merriam?
MERRIAM. What?
BENNIE. Why are we fighting?
MERRIAM. We're not fighting, we're simply holding a conversation, when people are expressing themselves, sometimes they get excited and . . .
BENNIE. (*Looks out window.*) Where are we?
MERRIAM. (*Also looking out window.*) Oh, oh, I think you missed your stop, Bennie, it's back there!

(*SHE pushes the buzzer. BENNIE jumps up automatically and runs to the door.*)

BENNIE. Write me, okay?
MERRIAM. Sure.
BENNIE. 'Bye.
MERRIAM. 'Bye.

(*BENNIE starts to get off the bus, then stops. HE hesitates a moment, then comes back to Merriam.*)

MERRIAM. What are you doing?
BENNIE. I'm not going.
MERRIAM. Bennie!?
BENNIE. I go too much. I gotta cut down.
MERRIAM. (*Smiling.*) You sound like a man with a bad habit.
BENNIE. Yeah.

(THEY look at each other for a long beat. BENNIE is still standing.)

BENNIE. Here. *(HE gives the roses to Merriam.)*

(THE bus hits a bump. BENNIE is thrown to one side.)

MERRIAM. You'd better sit down, it's dangerous standing on the bus . . .
BOTH. . . . especially *this* bus!

(BENNIE sits down beside Merriam.)

MERRIAM. Bennie?
BENNIE. Yeah?
MERRIAM. Thanks.
BENNIE. I didn't do anything.
MERRIAM. Yes you did. You gave me a hug.

(BENNIE reaches over and takes Merriam's hand. THEY smile at each other, then ride in silence holding hands. BENNIE looks at the roses and pulls off a petal. HE pops the petal into his mouth and starts chewing. HE nudges Merriam and indicates the roses.)

BENNIE. Enjoy.

(MERRIAM hesitates, then pulls off a petal and puts it into her mouth. SHE chews, likes the taste, plucks off a second petal and pops it into her mouth . . . as the LIGHTS slowly dim . . .)

THE END

COSTUME & PROP LIST

Act I, Scene 1 - Bus

Set Pieces	Props	Costumes	SFX
4 stools (Bus seats)	3 roses-B	Jacket-B Cap with ear muffs-B Galoshes-B Coat-M	Bus Car sounds

Act I, Scene 2 - Bus

Set Pieces	Props	Costumes	SFX
Same	3 carnations-B	Same	Same

Act I, Scene 3 - Chili Parlor

Set Pieces	Props	Costumes	SFX
2 stools Counter Sign: "Eat Chili and Grow"	Ketchup Salt & Pepper	Same	Restaurant music

Act I, Scene 4 - Bennie's Apartment

Set Pieces	Props	Costumes	SFX
Castle	Records	Same	Music (jazz
Stereo	Games		and ballad
Kitchen	Paintings		records)
table			
2 chairs			

Act I, Scene 5 - Bowling Alley

Set Pieces	Props	Costumes	SFX
Scoring	Martini	Jeans-B	Bowling
stand	glass	Baseball	alley
Ball return	Can of Coke	cap-B	
chute	Orange	Open shirt-B	
Rack	bowling	Sneakers-B	
w/bowling	ball	Sneakers-M	
balls		Slacks-M	
		Open blouse	
		-M	
			Music bridge
			to next
			scene

Act I, Scene 6 - Merriam's Apartment

Set Pieces	Props	Costumes	SFX
Couch	Box of	Suit & tie-B	Recording of
w/pillows	candy-B	Heels-M	Turandot
Coffee table	box of	Business	
Stereo stand	Kleenex-	suit-M	
Easy chair	M		

Act II, Scene 1 - Merriam's Apartment

Set Pieces	Props	Costumes	SFX
Same as I-6	2 coffee mugs	Robe/ slippers- M	Record of Carmina Burana
	Plate/sand- wich	Same as prev. scene-B	Swingle Singers
	Box of pills		
	Record jackets (incl one of Lawrence Welk's Golden Oldies		
	Deck of cards		

Act II, Scene 2 - Bennie's Apartment

Set Pieces	Props	Costumes	SFX
Same as I-4	Same as I-4	Shorts-B	Turandot
	Bag of food on paper plates	Jeans-B	
	Ironing board-B	T-shirt-B	
		Jacket-M	
		Slacks and blouse-M	

Act II, Scene 3 - Bus

Set Pieces	Props	Costumes	SFX
Same as I-1	3 roses	Sweater-B	Bus
		Same as II-2	

Backside, Sedum

Bus Seats

Act One, Scene One
Act One, Scene Two
Act Two, Scene Three

The Bus

Turn The Other Way!

The Chilli Parlour

Run, Eli, Catch You!

"Eat Chilli And Grow"
Sign

Spoons

Counter

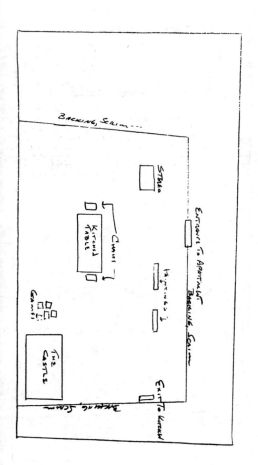

ACT ONE SCENE FOUR
ACT TWO SCENE TWO
DEANIE'S APARTMENT

... And I'll Catch You!

ACT ONE SCENE FIVE

THE BOWLING ALLEY

TURN, I'LL CATCH YOU!

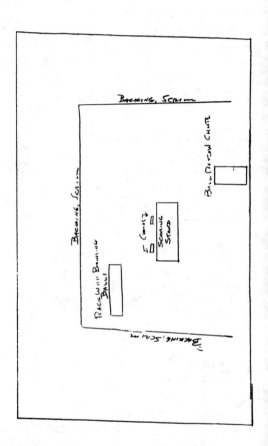

ACT ONE SCENE SIX
ACT TWO SCENE ONE
[MEGHAN'S APARTMENT]

JUMP, I'LL CATCH YOU!

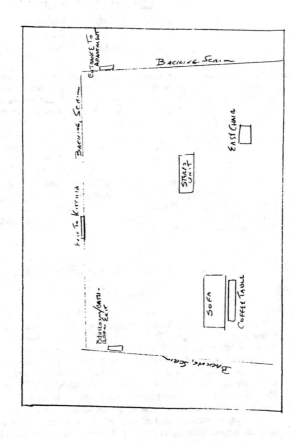

MIXED FEELINGS
(Little Theatre—Comedy)

Donald Churchill
m., 2 f., Int.

This is a riotous comedy about divorce, that ubiquitous, peculiar institution which so shapes practically everyone's life. Arthur and Norma, ex-spouses, live in separate apartments in the same building. Norma has second thoughts about her on-going affair with Arthur's best-friend; while Arthur isn't so sure he wants to continue *his* dalliance with Sonia, wife of a manufacturer with amusingly kinky sexual tastes (Dennis—the manufacturer—doesn't mind that his wife is having an affair; just so long as she continues to provide him with titillating accounts of it while he is dressed as a lady traffic cop). Most of Sonia's accounts are pure fiction, which seems to keep Dennis happy. Comic sparks are ignited into full-fledged farcical flames in the second act, when Dennis arrives in Arthur's flat for lessons in love from the legendary Arthur! "Riotous! A domestic laught romp! A super play. You'll laugh all the way home, I promise you.'—Eastbourne News. "Very funny ... a Churchill comedy that most people will thoroughly enjoy."—The Stage. Restricted New York City.

THE DECORATOR
(Little Theatre/Comedy)

Donald Churchill
m., 2 f., Int.

Much to her surprise, Marcia returns home to find that her flat has not been painted, as she arranged. In fact, the job hasn't even been started yet. There on the premises is the housepainter who is filling in for his ill colleague. As he begins work, there is a surprise visitor--the wife of the man with whom Marcia is having an affair, who has come to confront her nemesis and to exact her revenge by informing Marcia's husband of his wife's infidelity. Marcia is at her wit's end about what to do, until she gets a brilliant idea. It seems the housepainter is a part-time professional actor. Marcia hires him to impersonate her husband, Reggie, at the big confrontation later that day, when the wronged wife plans to return and spill the beans. Hilarity is piled upon hilarity as the housepainter, who takes his acting *very* seriously, portrays the absent Reggie. The wronged wife decides that the best way to get back at Marcia would be to sleep with her "husband" (the house painter), which is an ecstatic experience for them both. When Marcia learns that the housepainter/actor/husband has slept with her rival, she demands to have the opportunity to show the housepainter what *really* good sex is. "This has been the most amazing day of my life", says the sturdy painter, as Marcia leads him into her bedroom. "Irresistible."—London Daily Telegraph.

Other Publications for Your Interest

THE MAN WITH THE PLASTIC SANDWICH

(LITTLE THEATRE—COMEDY)

By ROGER KARSHNER

2 men, 2 women—Simple exterior

Walter Price, a "basic blue" individual, is thrown out of work after twenty years with the same firm. During an anxiety-laden period of job hunting and readjustment Walter attempts to find solace on a bench in an urban park. Here he is confronted by three engaging, provocative characters. First there is Ellie, a high-spirited ingenue who represents hope; then Haley, a distinguished hobo representing wisdom; and finally Lenore, a hooker who represents reality. Each encounter enlightens Walter, gives him perspective, and ultimately new purpose and direction. A very funny play with bittersweet moments and three dimensional characters. "You will laugh until your sides feel as if they will burst, until your eyes begin to water, until you are sure that one more clever line or witty exchange will send you into a laughing fit from which you may never recover."—Chicago Sun-Times. "This play is truly high comedy and I can't think of a soul who wouldn't love the off-beat characters portrayed in this 4-spoked comedic wheel."—Chicago Reporter/Progress Newspapers.

THE DREAM CRUST

(LITTLE THEATRE—DRAMA)

By ROGER KARSHNER

3 men, 3 women, 1 10-year-old boy —Interior

Named in the Bruns-Mantle Yearbook as one of America's Best Plays. Frank Haynes, an earth-loving farmer, has given up his hound-dogging and high times under the pressure of the family's admonition that "A man has got to get ahead." Haynes would be happy to do nothing but tend his farm and reap whatever profit it might generate. But he realizes that there are five mouths depending on him and the lure of big money available to him in a nearby big-city factory too great to ignore. Set against a backdrop of the land-locked Midwest, the play dramatizes a man's persistent, agonizing search for personal freedom and the sense of loss between father and son. "A moving portrait of a land-locked family that needs to be seen."—Variety. "The plays' spirit, its underlying warmth, particularly in the unspoken father-son relationship, creates a world that's identifiable and that breathes."—L.A. Herald-Examiner.

Other Publications for Your Interest

THE SQUARE ROOT OF LOVE
(ALL GROUPS—FOUR COMEDIES)
By DANIEL MELTZER

1 man, 1 woman—4 Simple Interiors

This full-length evening portrays four preludes to love—from youth to old age, from innocence to maturity. Best when played by a single actor and actress. **The Square Root of Love.** Two genius-level college students discover that Man (or Woman) does not live by intellectual pursuits alone . . . **A Good Time for a Change.** Our couple are now a successful executive and her handsome young male secretary. He has decided it's time for a change, and so has she . . . **The Battling Brinkmires.** George and Marsha Brinkmire, a middle-aged couple, have come to Haiti to get a "quickie" divorce. This one has a surprise ending . . . **Waiting For To Go.** We are on a jet waiting to take off for Florida. He's a retired plumbing contractor who thinks his life is over—she's a recent widow returning to her home in Hallandale. The play, and the evening, ends with a beginning . . . A success at off-off Broadway's Hunter Playwrights. Requires only minimal settings.   (#21314)

SNOW LEOPARDS
(LITTLE THEATRE—COMIC DRAMA)
By MARTIN JONES

2 women—Exterior

This haunting little gem of a play was a recent crowd-pleaser Off Off Broadway in New York City, produced by the fine StageArts Theatre Co. Set in Lincoln Park Zoo in Chicago in front of the snow leopards' pen, the play tells the story of two sisters from rural West Virginia. When we first meet Sally, she has run away from home to find her big sister Claire June, whose life Up North she has imagined to be filled with all the promise and hopes so lacking Down Home. Turns out, life in the Big City ain't all Sally and C.J. thought it would be: but Sally is going to stay anyway, and try to make her way. "Affecting and carefully crafted . . . a moving piece of work."—New York City Tribune. *Actresses take note*: this play is a treasure trove of scene and monologue material. *Producers take note*: the play may be staged simply and inexpensively.   (#21245)

Other Publications for Your Interest

THE CURATE SHAKESPEARE
AS YOU LIKE IT
(LITTLE THEATRE—COMEDY)

By DON NIGRO

4 men, 3 women—Bare stage

This extremely unusual and original piece is subtitled: "The record of one company's attempt to perform the play by William Shakespeare". When the very prolific Mr. Nigro was asked by a professional theatre company to adapt As You Like It so that it could be performed by a company of seven he, of course, came up with a completely original play about a rag-tag group of players comprised of only seven actors led by a dotty old curate who nonetheless must present Shakespeare's play; and the dramatic interest, as well as the comedy, is in their hilarious attempts to impersonate all of Shakespeare's multitude of characters. The play has had numerous productions nationwide, all of which have come about through word of mouth. We are very pleased to make this "underground comic classic" widely available to theatre groups who like their comedy wide open and theatrical. (#5742)

SEASCAPE WITH SHARKS
AND DANCER
(LITTLE THEATRE—DRAMA)

By DON NIGRO

1 man, 1 woman—Interior

This is a fine new play by an author of great talent and promise. We are very glad to be introducing Mr. Nigro's work to a wide audience with Seascape With Sharks and Dancer, which comes directly from a sold-out, critically acclaimed production at the world-famous Oregon Shakespeare Festival. The play is set in a beach bungalow. The young man who lives there has pulled a lost young woman from the ocean. Soon, she finds herself trapped in his life and torn between her need to come to rest somewhere and her certainty that all human relationships turn eventually into nightmares. The struggle between his tolerant and gently ironic approach to life and her strategy of suspicion and attack becomes a kind of war about love and creation which neither can afford to lose. In other words, this is quite an offbeat, wonderful love story. We would like to point out that the play also contains a wealth of excellent *monologue* and *scene material*. (#21060)

Other Publications for Your Interest

WITHDRAWN

CINDERELLA WALTZ
GROUND COMEDY
By D. NIGRO

...ssy Snow is trapped in a fairy tale world that is by turns funny and a little frightening, with her stepsisters Goneril and Regan, her demented stepmother, her lecherous father, a bewildered Prince, a fairy godmother who sings salty old sailor songs, a troll and a possibly homicidal village idiot. A play which investigates the archetypal origins of the ...nd charming ...brothers

(#5208)

...to cut
...tennis
...opular
...r in the
...esman,
...world
...es her
...de the

(20075)